SECRETS
OF THE
SKY

Library of Congress Catalog Card Number: 85-40923

ISBN 0-87406-078-8 (paper)
ISBN 0-87406-079-6 (lib. bdg.)

Printed in U.S.A.

SECRETS
OF THE
SKY

IAN RIDPATH

Willowisp
Press

CONTENTS

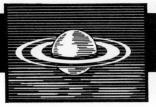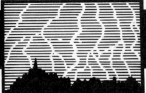

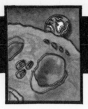

RAINBOWS
SPLITTING SUNLIGHT

It is a blustery spring afternoon. Rain clouds chase each other across the sky. As one shower clears, the Sun comes out—and a transparent multi-colored arch appears opposite it in the sky. We are witnessing a rainbow, one of the most beautiful sights in nature.

A rainbow is caused by sunlight shining on falling raindrops. Raindrops split up the Sun's light into colors as shown in the diagram. All the colors of the spectrum are visible in a rainbow: red, orange, yellow, green, blue, indigo and violet, with red on the outside and violet on the

inside of the arch. Sometimes, when the sunlight is strong, an outer rainbow, known as the secondary bow, can also be seen. In this, the order of colors is reversed, with violet on the outside and red on the inside.

For a rainbow to form, the raindrops must be opposite the Sun in the sky. The raindrops that cause a rainbow are usually about a mile (no more than a kilometer or two) away from the observer. Rainbows can also be seen in the spray from a waterfall or from a garden sprinkler.

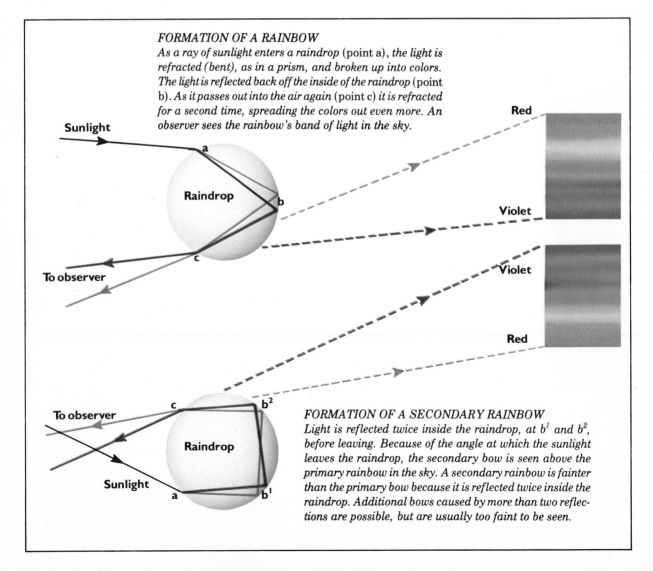

FORMATION OF A RAINBOW
As a ray of sunlight enters a raindrop (point a), the light is refracted (bent), as in a prism, and broken up into colors. The light is reflected back off the inside of the raindrop (point b). As it passes out into the air again (point c) it is refracted for a second time, spreading the colors out even more. An observer sees the rainbow's band of light in the sky.

FORMATION OF A SECONDARY RAINBOW
Light is reflected twice inside the raindrop, at b^1 and b^2, before leaving. Because of the angle at which the sunlight leaves the raindrop, the secondary bow is seen above the primary rainbow in the sky. A secondary rainbow is fainter than the primary bow because it is reflected twice inside the raindrop. Additional bows caused by more than two reflections are possible, but are usually too faint to be seen.

 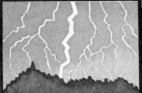  

Above: *Sun halo and mock Suns seen in Antarctica.*

HALOS

Rainbows are not the only optical effects caused by sunlight in the atmosphere. Most familiar of these other effects is a halo around the Sun, seen when the Sun is shining through a layer of high, thin cloud. Tiny ice crystals in the cloud act like little prisms, bending the Sun's light into a halo. A halo around the Sun is faintly colored, like a pale rainbow, being reddest on the inside and bluest on the outside. Similar halos can be seen around the Moon when viewed through high-altitude clouds.

Sometimes, at the edge of a Sun halo, brighter spots can be seen to the left and right of the Sun.

These spots are known as mock Suns, Sun dogs, or parhelia. They occur when the ice crystals in the cloud line up in a particular way, with their long axes vertical.

Legends of the rainbow

The sight of a gossamer rainbow appearing as if by magic in thin air has led to many myths and legends about it. In Scandinavia the rainbow was known as Bifrost, the bridge that connected Earth and heaven. A popular folk tale says that a pot of gold can be found at the end of the rainbow. Of course, a rainbow is not a real object but a form of optical illusion. As the observer approaches it, so the rainbow seems to move away. Hence, the end of a rainbow can never be reached. The pot of gold at the end of the rainbow is a symbol of something that is unattainable.

LIGHTNING

FLASH, THEN CRASH

A flash of lightning is an immense spark of electricity that jumps through several miles of air. At any one time more than 1,000 thunderstorms are active around the world, producing a global total of more than 100 lightning flashes each second!

A thunderstorm begins when large volumes of warm air rise and condense to form a towering thundercloud. The cloud becomes electrically charged with static electricity. The top of the cloud, which may reach a height of six miles (10 kilometers) or more, is positively charged, while the lower part of the cloud is negatively charged. Lightning occurs when the electric charge builds up to hundreds of millions of volts, sufficient to break down the insulating effect of the intervening air.

Most lightning takes place inside the cloud, producing what is known as sheet lightning. But spectacular effects occur when the electric spark jumps between the cloud and the ground, producing forked lightning. First, a faint line of light, known as the leader stroke, zigzags down from the cloud, electrically short-circuiting the cloud to the ground. A strong electrical current immediately surges upward from the ground to the cloud along the leader stroke's path, producing the brilliant return stroke. Therefore, the flash of light that we see as lightning actually travels upward, not downward, although it moves so quickly that its direction is impossible to see except with special high-speed photography. The energy released in each stroke of lightning is enough to keep a one-kilowatt electric fire burning for a week. Usually three or four further discharges occur up and down the same path before the flash ends one-tenth of a second after it began.

1. *Lightning begins when a faint, so-called leader stroke descends from an electrically charged cloud, short-circuiting the cloud to the ground.*

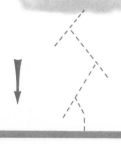

2. *A brilliant electrical discharge surges up from the ground to the cloud along the channel formed by the leader.*

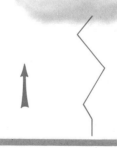

3. *After a brief, non-luminous period, another faint leader descends from the cloud to the ground along the same path.*

4. *Another return stroke surges from the ground to the cloud. The sequence in 3 and 4 may recur several times in rapid succession.*

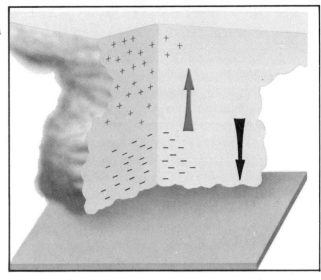

CROSS-SECTION THROUGH A THUNDERCLOUD
The top of the cloud collects a positive electrical charge, while the bottom of the cloud becomes negatively charged.

BALL LIGHTNING, ONE OF NATURE'S MYSTERIES

During a violent thunderstorm one summer's afternoon in 1975, a housewife was startled to see a bright blue ball of light appear in midair in her kitchen on the outskirts of Birmingham, England. The glowing ball, about four inches (about 10 centimeters) across, floated slowly toward her at waist height, giving off a crackling sound and a burning smell. As she brushed it away with her hand in alarm, it exploded with a bang. Where the ball of light had hit her, a hole was burned in her dress, and her hand was red and swollen.

She had encountered ball lightning, one of the most puzzling phenomena in nature. Scientists still do not fully understand ball lightning, but it is thought to be a pocket of electrified air. The fact that it can appear inside buildings makes it even odder.

Ball lightning is rare, but people who have seen it say that it is red, orange or blue in color, and can last anywhere from a few seconds to several minutes. One of the best sightings was made by a scientist on an airline flight during a thunderstorm. He saw a glowing blue-white ball, eight inches (20 centimeters) across emerge from the pilot's cabin and pass silently along the central aisle of the aircraft, vanishing from view at the rear. Ball lightning can be dangerous: in several cases glowing balls of light have been seen to enter oil tankers at sea or tank trucks transporting fuel, causing explosions.

How far away is the storm?

A lightning stroke heats the air through which it passes to 45,000°F, (25,000°C), four times the temperature of the surface of the Sun. The heated air expands rapidly outward, producing a thunderclap. Because sound travels more slowly than light, the thunder is heard after the lightning is seen. Count the number of seconds between seeing the flash of lightning and hearing the boom of thunder; then divide the number of seconds by five to obtain the distance to the storm in miles, or by three to get it in kilometers.

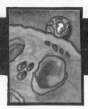

MIRAGES

REFLECTIONS IN THE AIR

Look along a road on a hot summer's day. The surface appears to be covered with puddles, although there is not really any water on the road. What you are seeing is a simple form of mirage, the despair of thirsty travelers in the desert.

Mirages are caused when light is bent as it passes through layers of air of different temperatures. For example, a layer of warm air forms just above the surface of a flat road on a sunny day. Light entering this layer of air from above is bent upward as though by a lens, so that the light becomes visible to a person further along the road. The pools of water that seem to lie on the road are actually images of the sky! Surrounding objects can appear to be reflected in the pools. Such mirages commonly form over the flat sands of deserts, where they create the illusion of a welcoming oasis.

An opposite type of mirage occurs over water when warm air lies above cooler, denser air. In this case an object below the horizon, such as a ship, will be seen apparently floating in the air. Perhaps this is the origin of the legend of the Flying Dutchman, a phantom ship reportedly sighted on the seas by sailors in olden days.

In another example of mirages seen over water, the image of people on the far shore of a lake can be magnified so that they appear to be standing in the middle of the lake. This gives the impression that the people are walking on the water. Mirages of this kind may have given rise to stories of holy men who could perform such miraculous feats.

Mirages can also be seen over snow. In 1906 the polar explorer Robert Peary reported sighting snow-clad summits above the ice horizon, which he believed heralded an immense, undiscovered land in the Artic. It was given the name Crocker Land. But other explorers who tried to reach it found that Crocker Land did not exist. It was a mirage of the type known as Fata Morgana, in which the Earth's surface, land or water, appears raised upward into a variety of fantastic shapes, from mountains to castles.

Above: *Mirages occur not only in the desert but also over ice, as in this photograph taken in Antarctica.*

Left: *When a layer of warm air lies above cooler air, light rays are bent downward, so that the object appears to be suspended above the horizon.*

Mirage

Observer

Warm air

Cool air

Far left: *A layer of warm air close to the ground bends light rays upward, so that an observer sees what appears to be reflections in a pool of water underneath a direct view of the object.*

These giraffes appear to be walking on water as the result of a mirage.

Fata Morgana

Fata Morgana is the name sometimes given to a mirage in which the image of the distant sea or land is distorted into the shape of mountains, towers and arches, all seeming to float in the air. Fata Morgana is Italian for the name Morgan the Fairy, a character in the legends of King Arthur who had the magical power of making castles in the air. The Fata Morgana type of mirage is commonly seen over the Straits of Messina between Italy and Sicily. This one (right) was in the Sahara.

HURRICANES AND TORNADOES

THE FURY OF NATURE

Hurricanes are the most destructive storms in nature. Spotting them and tracking them is one of the most important tasks of meteorologists. In November 1970 an estimated 500,000 people were killed when a hurricane swept over low-lying islands in the Bay of Bengal. Most of the Australian city of Darwin was destroyed in 1974 by a hurricane.

In the Pacific, such storms are called typhoons. Elsewhere they are known as tropical cyclones. But all these names mean one thing: an immensely powerful whirling mass of air up to 625 miles (1,000 kilometers) in diameter in which winds reach speeds of at least 75 miles (120 kilometers) per hour and can be as high as 190 miles (300 kilometers) per hour, sufficient to knock down trees, lift off roofs, and flatten some buildings.

About 50 to 60 hurricanes occur around the world each year. The main danger areas include the north-west Pacific, the Bay of Bengal, the south-eastern United States and the Caribbean. A hurricane begins as a depression (a body of low-pressure air) over a warm ocean. Warm, moist air flows into the depression, feeding more energy into the growing storm to stir its winds to ever-higher speeds. Hurricanes spiral counter-clockwise in the northern hemisphere, and clockwise in the southern hemisphere.

After forming at sea, hurricanes are pushed inland, by the local wind systems, causing immense devastation. Towering waves whipped up at sea pound the coastline. In addition to the tempestuous winds of the hurricane, the storm releases torrential rain, causing flooding. At the center of the hurricane is the eye, 6 to 30 miles (10 to 50 kilometers) across, bounded by towering walls of clouds which reach over six miles (10 kilometers) high. Around the eye of the hurricane the strongest winds rage and the heaviest rains fall. But in the eye itself, relative calm prevails. Light winds blow and the Sun may even come out for a

Left: Destruction caused by a hurricane that hit Ocean City, Maryland in 1962. Below: Eye of Hurricane Gracie seen from the air off the coast of South Carolina.

 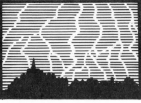  

short while. After half an hour or so the eye passes, and the hurricane-force winds return.

Over land, a hurricane is deprived of the warm, moist air from the ocean that powers it, so the storm blows itself out after a few days. Orbiting weather satellites keep a permanent watch on the Earth so that no hurricane escapes their detection. The advance warning that satellites give of hurricanes forming out at sea saves lives and property.

The fastest winds on Earth are found in twisting funnels of air known as tornadoes. A tornado descends from a severe thunderstorm to scour a trail of destruction over the countryside below. Over 600 tornadoes a year are reported in the United States, their most common breeding ground, but they also occur in many other parts of the world. "Twister" is their popular name. If a tornado occurs over the ocean, it is known as a waterspout. A whirlwind is a less severe form of tornado.

Sometimes several tornadoes can descend from a storm cloud at the same time. Each cloudy column of air spins at speeds of up to 600 miles (1,000 kilometers) per hour. The tornado's high-speed winds, plus the low pressure at its furiously twisting center, destroy everything in its path. A tornado is usually only a few hundred meters in diameter, although some over half a mile (one kilometer) wide have been known. The force of the tornado's winds lifts animals, rocks, cars and people into the air, and flattens buildings in its path. The trail of a tornado can extend anywhere from a few to hundreds of miles. Fortunately, a tornado's passage is rapid, lasting only a few minutes in any one place.

Right: *A waterspout endangers small boats off the Costa Brava in Spain.* Below: *Descending from a storm cloud, a tornado forms a twisting funnel of terror in North Dakota in 1978.*

STONEHENGE

PREHISTORIC CALENDAR OR ANCIENT TEMPLE?

On a windswept plain in southern England lies one of the most famous, yet mysterious monuments in the world—Stonehenge. It was built thousands of years ago by prehistoric people. But what was its purpose—an observatory, a place of worship, or even a kind of Stone Age computer for predicting eclipses of the Sun and Moon?

Archaeologists have found that Stonehenge was built in several stages. The ring of giant standing stones which make the monument so impressive today was not part of the original structure. The first version of Stonehenge, built about 4,800 years ago, consisted of a circular ditch and bank nearly 330 feet (100 meters) in diameter, with an opening to the north-east. This opening lies in the direction in which the Sun is seen to rise on the longest day of the year in the northern hemisphere, June 21. On this day each year the Sun rises at its northernmost point on the horizon, which makes it an ideal point from which to calculate a calendar that would have told the local farmers when to reap and when to sow. Out-side the circular ditch and bank was placed a large stone, still standing, known as the Heel Stone. Anyone at the center of Stonehenge on Mid-summer Day (about June 21) sees the Sun rise over the Heel Stone.

Inside the circular ditch and bank lie a rect-angle of four small stones, known as the Station Stones, which could have been used to sight important rising and setting positions of the Sun and Moon. The Mark I version of Stonehenge seems to have been built by people who kept a careful watch on the sky and who used the monu-ment as a calendar and observatory.

Also inside the earthwork bank of the Mark I Stonehenge is a puzzling ring of 56 holes, known as the Aubrey Holes after their 17th-century discoverer John Aubrey. Their purpose is un-known, but some astronomers have suggested that the builders of Stonehenge could have moved markers around the Aubrey circle to re-present the motion of the Sun and Moon and hence to predict eclipses. Not many scientists

Left: *Sighting lines at Stonehenge point to important rising positions of the Sun and Moon.* Below: *The massive arches of the sarsen-stone circle frame the Heel Stone beyond.*

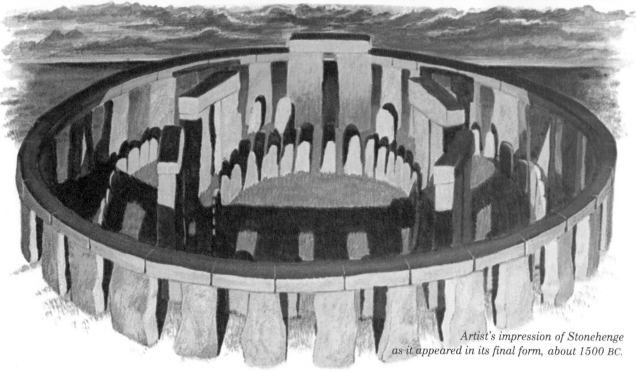

*Artist's impression of Stonehenge
as it appeared in its final form, about 1500 BC.*

agree with this theory.

After 700 years, Stonehenge entered a major period of reconstruction, during which the famous large standing stones, were dragged to Stonehenge from the Marlborough Downs, about 20 miles (about 30 kilometers) to the north. One set of sarsen stones was erected in a circle 100 feet (30 meters) in diameter, with another set of sarsen stones inside it in the form of a horseshoe. The largest of these stones weighs 45 tons. Transporting them and erecting them was a major feat of prehistoric engineering.

Construction at Stonehenge finished around 1500 BC. By then the original purpose of the monument as a calendar and observatory had almost certainly been replaced by a religious function. In its final version, Stonehenge seems to have been a prehistoric temple or cathedral, possibly dedicated to worship of the Sun and Moon. What strange rites went on in that circle at the first glimmer of the midsummer sunrise or under the cold light of the full Moon we will never know. The stones are silent.

Ancient observatories

Stonehenge is not the only example of a prehistoric observatory. Throughout Britain and parts of Europe there are hundreds of sites where standing stones were set up in rings or lines. As at Stonehenge, many of these monuments are aligned toward important astronomical points such as the rising of the midsummer Sun. An example of such a monument is at Callanish on the Isle of Lewis in the Outer Hebrides. Callanish (seen here at midsummer sunrise) is known as the Scottish Stonehenge.

METEORS AND METEORITES

SPACE DUST AND DEBRIS

In the early hours of November 17, 1966, astronomers in the United States saw an incredible sight: stars appeared to be cascading from the sky like snowflakes. The astronomers were lucky enough to be witnessing a rare and spectacular shower of shooting stars.

Despite their name, shooting stars are not stars at all. They are actually specks of dust from space, about the size of grains of sand, burning up by friction as they plunge at high speed into the Earth's atmosphere. The proper name for them is meteors. Normally, on any clear night several meteors can be seen each hour. They appear as sudden streaks of light darting across part of the sky, usually vanishing in a second or less.

Such random meteors are termed sporadic. But at certain times each year the Earth encounters swarms of dust that give rise to meteor showers, during which dozens of meteors can flash out each hour in a thrilling celestial firework display. Unlike sporadic meteors, which come from any direction in space, the meteors of a shower radiate from a specific area of sky, from which the shower takes its name. For example, the bright Perseid meteors of mid-August radiate from the constellation of Perseus, the Orionids of October come from Orion, and so on.

Meteor showers are caused by dust shed from comets orbiting the Sun. When the Earth passes close to a comet, exceptional displays of meteors can occur, such as the great Leonid storm over the United States in 1966, when up to 100,000 meteors per hour were seen pouring from the constellation of Leo. Comet Tempel-Tuttle, which gives rise to the Leonid meteors, will be close to the Earth again in 1999, so another great Leonid storm may be expected then.

The specks of dust that cause meteors burn up

at a height of 60 miles (100 kilometers), so there is no chance of being hit on the head by one! But occasionally much larger lumps of rock or metal

Trails of light, caused by tiny specks of dust from space burning up in the atmosphere, flashed out at the rate of 100,000 a minute during the great Leonid meteor storm of November 17, 1966.

16

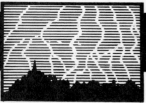

Above: *This great crater 0.75 miles (1.2 kilometers) wide, was blasted out of the Arizona desert by an iron meteorite 25,000 years ago. White spots on the crater floor were caused by drilling.*
Left: *The heaviest meteorite yet found weighs 60 tons and lies where it fell more than a million years ago at Grootfontein in Namibia. Weathering has reduced its original weight by about half.*

enter the Earth's atmosphere and reach the ground. These are known as meteorites. They are debris left over from the formation of the planets.

If a meteorite is moving quickly enough when it hits the ground it can blast out a gigantic crater. In the desert of northern Arizona, lies a crater 0.75 miles (1.2 kilometers) across that was formed about 25,000 years ago by a meteorite. The meteorite, which was made of iron, is estimated to have weighed 250,000 tons; most of it was vaporized in the heat of the impact.

Most meteorites are much smaller than this, and are usually slowed down by the Earth's atmosphere before they reach the ground, although they can still cause damage. In 1954 a woman in Alabama was bruised by a meteorite that crashed through the roof of her house and hit her on the hip. She is the only person known to have been struck by a meteorite.

About 500 meteorites hit the Earth each year, but most of these land in the oceans or remote areas and are never found. The heaviest known meteorite, made of iron, weighs 60 tons and lies where it fell in prehistoric times in Namibia, southwest Africa.

AURORAE

NEON LIGHTS IN THE SKY

A red glow in the sky over Ancient Rome one night led the Emperor Tiberius to think that the nearby port of Ostia at the mouth of the river Tiber was burning down. He sent out a team of firefighters, but it turned out that there was no blaze. The glare was caused, not by a fire, but by an eerie natural effect known as the aurora (the plural is aurorae), in which the Earth's upper atmosphere glows like a colorful neon tube. Aurorae have been interpreted in the past as ghostly spirits or portents of doom. In fact, they are a sign that the Earth is being bombarded by high-speed atomic particles from space.

A common type of aurora looks like a greenish-yellow arch or curtain, stretching east and west for thousands of miles, often with folds that seem to move and shimmer. Other types of aurorae appear like bands of light or are simply a general fiery red glow like the one seen by the Emperor Tiberius. They occur from 60 miles (100 kilometers) up to about 600 miles (about 1,000 kilometers) above the Earth.

Normally aurorae appear only near the Arctic and Antarctic circles. They are a familiar sight to people in Alaska, northern Canada, Scotland, Norway and Sweden. Only occasionally is the ethereal glow of the aurora visible over a wider area, which is why the Emperor Tiberius was fooled. In the northern hemisphere the aurora is known as the Aurora Borealis, or northern lights; in the southern hemisphere it is called the Aurora Australis, or southern lights.

Left: Solar flare, seen erupting at the Sun's edge, flings atomic particles into space that reach the Earth to cause aurorae. Below: A glowing aurora produces a beautiful effect like folded drapery over Antarctica.

Surprisingly, we must look to storms on the Sun for the cause of aurorae. Eruptions, called flares, on the Sun's boiling surface throw out streams of atomic particles which speed through space at up to 600 miles (1,000 kilometers) per second, taking about two days to cross the 93 million mile (150 million kilometer) gap to the Earth. In ways still not fully understood by scientists, the atomic particles enter the magnetic shell around the Earth, known as the magnetosphere. The magnetosphere acts like a gigantic television tube, focusing the beams of atomic particles toward the Earth's polar regions where they hit the Earth's upper atmosphere, causing the oxygen and nitrogen atoms to glow colorfully.

VAN ALLEN BELTS

When the first American satellites went into orbit around the Earth in 1958 they found something startlingly unexpected: two doughnut-shaped rings of atomic particles are trapped in the magnetic field of the Earth. These are named the Van Allen belts, after the American scientist James Van Allen who designed the equipment that detected them. Astronauts who orbit the Earth must fly underneath the lower Van Allen belt, at heights of no more than a few hundred miles, to keep clear of harmful radiation from the atomic particles in the belt. Going to the Moon they pass through the Van Allen belts so quickly that the radiation they receive is no more than from a dental X ray.

The lower of the two Van Allen belts lies between 600 and 3,100 miles (1,000 and 5,000 kilometers) above the Earth, and contains protons and electrons. The outer belt lies between 9,300 and 15,500 miles (15,000 and 25,000 kilometers) above the Earth's equator, but dips lower around the poles. This outer belt mostly contains electrons. The atomic particles in the Van Allen belts come both from the Earth's upper atmosphere and from the Sun.

The Van Allen belts are caught inside the magnetosphere, which cocoons our planet. On the side facing the Sun, the edge of the magnetosphere lies about 37,000 miles (about 60,000 kilometers) from the Earth, but on the side away from the Sun it is drawn out into a long pear-shaped tail that extends for millions of miles into space.

MAGNETOSPHERE AND VAN ALLEN BELTS
Our planet's magnetic field encloses the Earth in a magnetic bubble called the magnetosphere. The Van Allen belts are swarms of atomic particles trapped inside the magnetosphere. Around the outside of the magnetosphere sweeps the solar wind, a stream of atomic particles from the Sun.

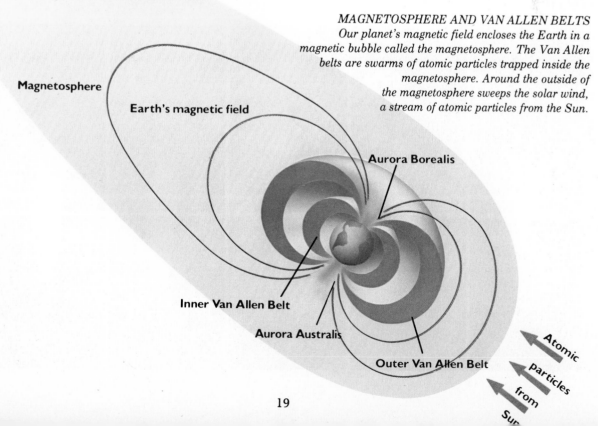

Magnetosphere

Earth's magnetic field

Aurora Borealis

Inner Van Allen Belt

Aurora Australis

Outer Van Allen Belt

Atomic particles from Sun

COMETS
INTERPLANETARY WANDERERS

A bright comet is a rare and awesome apparition that appears in the sky like a cosmic specter. From its head, a rounded misty patch, extends a diaphanous tail, often shaped like a fan or a curved sword. The whole comet glows ethereally. No wonder that throughout history people regarded comets as terrifying omens of evil.

Astronomers now know that comets are interplanetary wanderers made of frozen gas and dust. They loop around the Sun on highly elongated orbits, usually taking many thousands of years to complete one circuit. When far from the Sun, in the icy reaches of deep space, a comet is frozen into a solid block like a dirty snowball, only about half a mile (about one kilometer) across. But as it approaches the Sun it starts to warm up and expand. The gases evaporate and the dust is released, forming the comet's fuzzy head and its long flowing tail. Despite the appearance of high-speed motion that the tail gives, a comet does not whiz across the sky, but gradually changes its position and appearance from night to night.

Comets are thought to exist in their billions in a cloud far beyond the known planets about six trillion miles (about 10 trillion kilometers) from the Sun, where they have remained since the formation of the solar system. Occasionally the gravitational pull of a passing star nudges some of these comets out of the cloud and on to a new orbit that brings them in toward the Sun. As a comet approaches the Sun it brightens and can be followed by telescopes on Earth for several weeks or months. Only once in every few years does one come along that is bright enough to be visible to the naked eye.

Once a comet has rounded the Sun it heads off back into space again. Most comets do not return for thousands or millions of years, but some comets enter shorter orbits that bring them back to the Sun more frequently. The comet with the shortest known orbit, Encke's Comet, moves

Below: Development of the tail of Comet Arend-Roland over a six-day period in 1957. From left: April 26, April 27, April 29, April 30, May 1.

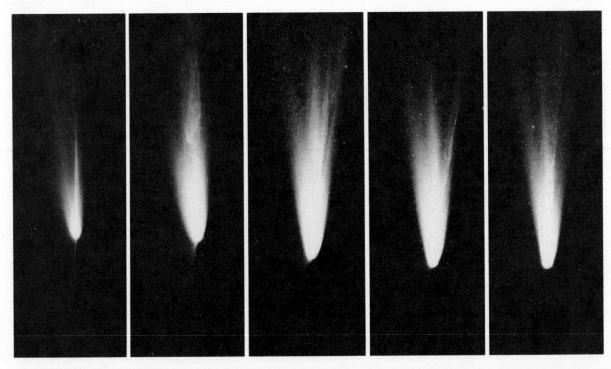

once around the Sun every 3.3 years, but it has lost so much of its gas and dust that it is too faint to be seen without a telescope. Ten or more comets may be visible through telescopes on Earth each year. Some of these are new discoveries, but others are known comets returning to the vicinity of the Sun. Over 1,000 comets are known, and more are being discovered all the time, often by amateur astronomers who

Above: *Comet Bennett stretched its beautiful tail across the sky in 1970.* Inset: *Three stages in the breakup of the head of Comet West in 1976, photographed on March 8, March 14, and March 18.*

specifically keep watch for them. Anyone who discovers a comet has it named after them—a form of immortality written in the sky.

What is a comet made of?

A comet has two main parts: the head and the tail. The head consists of a glowing sphere of gas and dust about 60,000 miles (about 100,000 kilometers) in diameter known as the *coma,* at the center of which lies the tiny *nucleus,* only a few kilometers across. The nucleus is made of rock and ice, and is the only solid part of a comet. The nucleus releases the gas and dust that forms the coma and the tail.

A comet's tail consists of gas and dust that has been blown away from the head by the Sun's radiation. The dust particles from the comet spread out into a fan-shaped tail several million kilometers long, while the gas particles make a tail that is straighter and can stretch much further, up to 60 million miles (100 million kilometers) or more. Comet tails always point away from the Sun, no matter in which direction the comet is traveling.

Despite their immense size, comets are very insubstantial objects. It would take a trillion comets to equal the mass of the Earth.

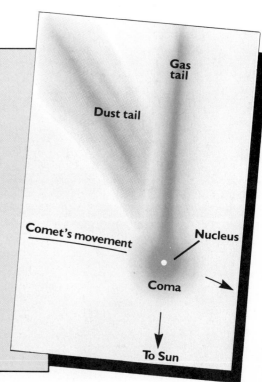

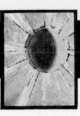

HALLEY'S COMET

ONCE EVERY 76 YEARS

The most famous comet in history, Halley's Comet, is returning to the inner solar system in 1985–86. It is being met by a flotilla of five space probes, two from Japan, two from the Soviet Union and one from Europe. In addition, it is the subject of intense scrutiny from observatories around the world, including instruments being carried about the Space Shuttle. Halley's Comet has been chosen as the target of this unprecedented effort because it is big, bright, and its return could be predicted well in advance. Astronomers hope that these detailed studies will help answer questions about comets in general, including their exact composition, origin, and the nature of the almost invisible central nucleus.

Halley's Comet orbits the Sun every 76 years on average, although this figure can vary from 74 to 79 years. The comet's path takes it from about 55 million miles (90 million kilometers) distance from the Sun (between the orbits of Mercury and Venus) to over 3,000 million miles (5,000 million kilometers) from the Sun (beyond the orbit of Neptune). It was first seen as far back as 240 BC. The comet appeared in 1066 shortly before the Battle of Hastings, and is shown on the Bayeux Tapestry. After another appearance in 1301 the Italian artist Giotto di Bondone depicted it in his painting *The Adoration of the Magi*. Giotto's name has now been given to the European space probe to Halley's Comet.

On its last appearance in 1910 the Earth actually passed through the tail of Halley's Comet, an event that caused widespread public alarm. In fact, the encounter had no noticeable effects on either the Earth or on the comet.

Left: *The elliptical orbit of Halley's Comet around the Sun.* Below: *The European Space Agency's probe Giotto. It is targeted to fly through the comet's head, taking photographs and samples of the material of which the comet is made. The probe and the comet will zip toward each other at the incredible speed of 150,000 miles (240,000 kilometers) per hour. Although protected by a dust shield, Giotto will probably be destroyed once it enters the comet's head.*

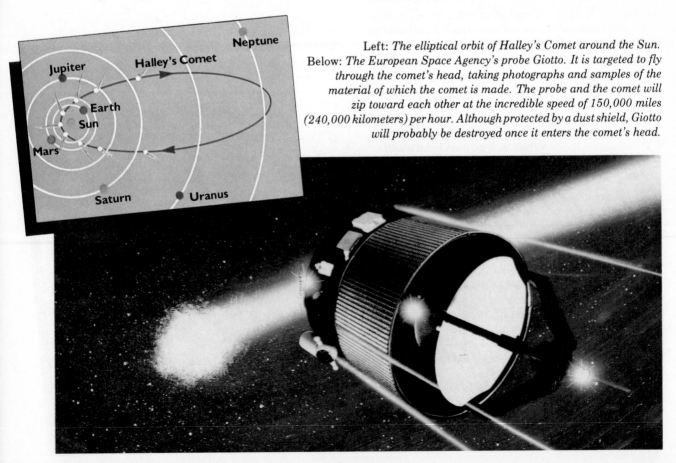

WHERE TO SEE HALLEY'S COMET

At its return in 1985–86 Halley's Comet will come no closer to the Earth than 38 million miles (60 million kilometers). It will not put on a very impressive show this time, at least for observers in the northern hemisphere. The best place to observe the comet at its brightest will be the southern hemisphere.

Observers in the northern hemisphere will get their first glimpse of Halley's Comet in small telescopes in November 1985, when it will lie in the constellation of Taurus. It should be visible in binoculars in the south-western evening sky in December 1985 and January 1986, although it is unlikely to be visible to the naked eye except in clear, dark skies away from towns.

In late January the comet will vanish behind the Sun, reappearing in the morning sky at the end of February, low on the eastern horizon before sunrise. When at its brightest in early April observers in the southern hemisphere will see the comet and its long tail almost overhead at dawn. But it will then lie too far south to be seen from mid-northern hemisphere latitudes.

As it recedes from the Sun and fades, Halley's Comet will move northward again. By the end of May binoculars will be required to keep track of the comet as it returns to the cold, dark reaches of the outer solar system, not to return again until the year 2062.

Above: *Halley's Comet, shown on the Bayeux Tapestry at its appearance in 1066. It is being pointed out to King Harold of England as a bad omen for the forthcoming Battle of Hastings. William the Conqueror and the Normans defeated the English in the battle and Harold himself was killed. The 11th-century Bayeux Tapestry is an embroidered strip of linen which depicts the Norman Conquest in about 70 scenes.*

How Halley's Comet got its name

Halley's Comet takes its name from the English astronomer Edmond Halley, who calculated its orbit in 1705. He noted that the orbits of the comets seen in 1682, 1607 and 1531 were all remarkably similar, and he guessed that these were all appearances of the same comet moving around the Sun every 75 to 76 years. He predicted that it would return in 1758. Sure enough, on Christmas night 1758 it was seen again, and it passed closest to the Sun in March 1759. Halley did not live to see the prediction fulfilled, but since then the comet has been given his name.

SPACE JUNK

LEFTOVERS FROM THE SPACE RACE

NASA space controllers watched nervously as their Skylab space station spiralled back toward Earth in July 1979. Skylab, the largest object ever put into orbit, had been empty since the last astronauts left in February 1974. Now, the drag of the Earth's outer atmosphere had slowed it down so much that is was about to fall out of orbit, raining hundreds of glowing fragments, some weighing a ton or more, onto the Earth below. But on one could predict where the bits would come down.

As luck would have it, Skylab's last revolution of the Earth, its 34,981st, passed over the South Atlantic and Indian Oceans. Most of the disintegrating space station fell into the sea, but not all. At Perth, Western Australia, eyewitnesses saw "sparks whirling everywhere" in the night sky as the last remains of Skylab blazed through the air above them, creating loud sonic booms and dropping fragments onto the Nullarbor Plain east of the town of Kalgoorlie. A rancher in the area reported "windmilling sounds" as pieces seemed to fall around him, followed by a burning smell.

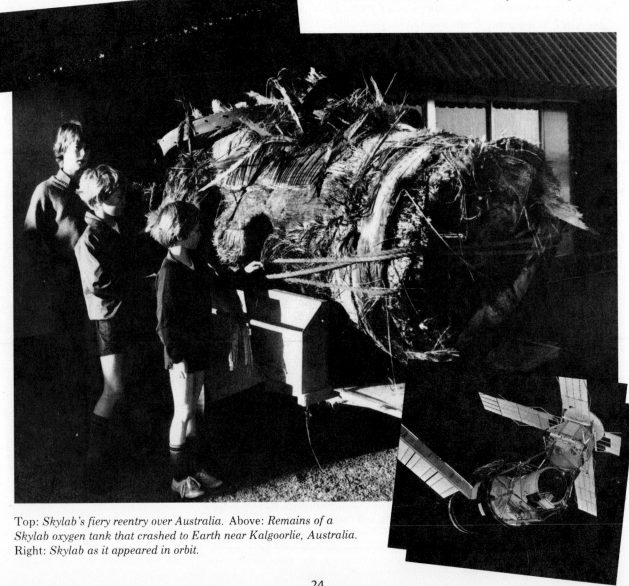

Top: *Skylab's fiery reentry over Australia.* Above: *Remains of a Skylab oxygen tank that crashed to Earth near Kalgoorlie, Australia.* Right: *Skylab as it appeared in orbit.*

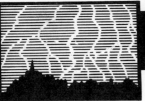

The largest pieces found included part of a docking port six feet (two meters) long by three feet (one meter) wide, some oxygen tanks, and the door from a film vault. Skylab's descent proved a bonus for one young Western Australian, who flew to California with some charred pieces of Skylab to collect a reward of $10,000 offered by a newspaper, the San Francisco *Examiner.*

At any one time there are many thousands of man-made objects in orbit around the Earth. These range from small pieces of debris the size of a pebble to complete satellites and discarded rocket stages as big as a bus. Scarcely a day goes by without some piece of space junk entering the atmosphere. Mostly these burn up harmlessly, but occasionally some pieces survive, and Skylab was not the first example.

A major scare occurred in January 1978 when a Soviet nuclear-powered spacecraft, Cosmos 954, crashed in northwestern Canada, spilling radioactive debris over a wide area. Fortunately, the region in which the pieces landed was uninhabited, but the clean-up operation cost the Canadian government over $10 million, of which the Soviet government eventually paid over $9 million. Under international law, whoever launches a spacecraft is responsible for any damage it may cause.

As early as 1962, a 20-pound (10-kilogram) piece of the Soviet Sputnik 4 landed on a street in Manitowoc, Wisconsin. In 1968 a window of a house in Southend, Essex, England was broken by a piece of a reentering Russian rocket. The Soviet satellite Cosmos 316 scattered a trail of debris totalling hundreds of pounds over Kansas, Oklahoma and Texas in August 1970. Two French farmers had a lucky escape in 1978 when a 45-pound (20-kilogram) lump of a Russian rocket fell into a potato field near them. The greenskeeper at the golf course in Eastbourne, Sussex, England, was surprised to find a nineteenth hole one morning in 1979. Again, a fragment from a Russian rocket was the culprit.

As the number of objects in space goes up, so the chances of a serious accident are increasing. Damage to people or property by reentering space junk could occur in the next few years.

The Soviet nuclear-powered satellite Cosmos 954 showered radioactive debris over Canada's North West Territories in 1978. Searchers found numerous fragments, such as this pipe-shaped object on the surface of the Great Slave Lake (above) and some metal rods at a site near the Thelon River (right).

TIDES AND PHASES OF THE MOON

PULLED THIS WAY AND THAT

Every day the waters of the Earth rise and fall in rhythmic response to the gravitational attractions of the Moon and Sun. Although both the Moon and the Sun cause tides, the Moon has the greater effect because it is much closer to us than the Sun.

To understand how tides occur, imagine that the Earth is entirely covered with water and the Moon alone is pulling on it. The water of the Earth forms into two bulges: one is on the side facing the Moon where the Moon's gravitational attraction is strongest, and the other is on the opposite side, where the Moon's gravitational attraction is least. A similar tidal effect is caused by the gravitational pull of the Sun, but it has less than half the effect of the Moon.

When the Moon and Sun are pulling in line, which happens every two weeks, their effects add up to make the tides particularly high. These are known as spring tides. When the Moon and Sun pull at right angles the tides are much less pronounced. These are known as neap tides. (Neap is an Old English word of uncertain origin.)

Usually each place on Earth has two tides a day as the Earth rotates under the two bulges of water. The time of high tide gets later by about 50 minutes each day, a result of the Moon's movement in its orbit around the Earth. If the Sun alone were involved, the tides would rise and fall by only about one-third as much as they actually do, and they would recur at the same time each day.

Tides vary markedly in height from place to place, depending on the local coastline. The Bay of Fundy on the Atlantic coast of Canada is famous for its extreme tides, which have a range of more than 50 feet (15 meters) between high and low.

Friction, caused by the tides as they flow over the sea botton, is slowing down the spin of the Earth like a brake. As a result, the length of the day is gradually increasing, by 0.0016 seconds per century. The amount is tiny, but it adds up: in 225 million years' time, for instance, there will be 25 hours in a day!

Tides in the Bay of Fundy, Canada, are extreme, as seen in these photographs below. Sea level can vary by more than 50 feet (15 meters) between low (below left) *and high tide* (below right).

PHASES OF THE MOON

The Moon looks different each night. It goes through an endlessly repeating cycle of phases from a crescent to a half, to full, and then back again. The phases are caused as the Moon orbits the Earth each month.

When the Moon lies between us and the Sun, all its sunlit side is turned away from us so that the Moon cannot be seen. This is new Moon. As the Moon moves around its orbit, increasing amounts of its sunlit side become visible: first a crescent in the evening sky, then a half (also known as first quarter), and then the three-quarters phase known as gibbous. The fully illuminated Moon lies opposite the Sun in the sky, and rises as the Sun sets. After full Moon, the sequence of phases reverses itself, through third quarter back to new. When the phase of the Moon is increasing, it is said to be waxing. When the phase is decreasing, the Moon is said to be waning.

The tidal barrage in the Rance Estuary, France which uses the flow of the tides to generate electricity.

TIDES

Earth   **Moon**

1

1. *The Moon's gravitational pull on the Earth is strongest along the line joining their centers.*

2   **B**   **A**   **C**   **Moon**

Earth

2. *The gravitational pull of the Moon (shown by the arrows) is stronger at A than at B, with the result that the water on that side of the Earth runs toward the Moon, forming a bulge. At C the gravitational attraction of the Moon is less than it is at B, so on that side of the Earth the water runs away from the Moon, forming another bulge.*

3   **New Moon**   **Sun**

Full Moon

3. *When the Moon and Sun pull in line, as happens at new Moon and full Moon, tides are highest. These are spring tides.*

First quarter

4   **Sun**

Last quarter

4. *When Sun and Moon pull at right angles, tides are least. These are neap tides.*

THE MOON

OUR NEAREST NEIGHBOR IN SPACE

The Moon, our nearest neighbor in space, is an airless and waterless ball of rock 2,160 miles (3,476 kilometers) in diameter, one-quarter the width of the Earth. It lies 239,000 miles (384,400 kilometers) away, a distance that light and radio waves jump in little more than a second, but which astronauts in spacecraft take three days to cross. The Moon is the only other world on which humans have walked. Astronauts have brought back samples of its rocks for study by scientists on Earth. You can use simple binoculars to view the ancient scars of craters and lava plains on its rugged surface.

To the naked eye the Moon appears dotted with dark patches that form the familiar Man-in-the-Moon pattern. In reality, these dark areas are lowland plains known as the Moon's "seas," filled not with water but with lava that oozed out from the Moon's interior billions of years ago. These dry seas are given fanciful Latin names such as Mare Tranquillitatis (Sea of Tranquillity) or Oceanus Procellarum (Ocean of Storms). The lunar seas are much smoother than the bright lunar highlands, which are a jumble of mountains and craters.

The largest craters on the Moon are 60 miles (100 kilometers) or more in diameter, enough to swallow a major city on Earth. They are named after famous scientists of the past. The craters are thought to have been formed by meteorites that crashed into the Moon long ago. Some craters are surrounded by rays of pulverized rock thrown out in the meteorite's impact.

Because the Moon keeps the same face turned toward the Earth all the time, no one had ever seen the Moon's far side before the spacecraft were sent. They showed that the far side of the Moon consists mostly of bright, heavily cratered uplands, with few dark lowland plains.

Below: *One small step: a footprint in the lunar dust left by the first man on the Moon.* Bottom: *Apollo 17 astronaut Harrison Schmitt is dwarfed by a boulder while exploring the Moon.*

Much of what we know about the Moon has come from study of the 840 pounds (380 kilograms) of rocks and soil brought back from the six landings made by American Apollo astronauts between 1969 and 1972. The Moon's surface turned out to be over 3,000 million years old, far more ancient than most of the Earth's surface. As expected, the lunar seas were filled with lava like that from volcanoes on Earth. The solidified lava has been worn down into dust by the impact of meteorites over thousands of millions of years.

One puzzle that the Apollo landings did not solve was the origin of the Moon. Did it form side by side with the Earth, was it a separate body that was caught by Earth's gravity, or did the Moon split off from the Earth? Most astronomers prefer the first explanation, but no one knows for sure.

Whatever the case, the rocks reveal that the Moon was born 4,600 million years ago, at the same time as the Earth and the rest of the solar system. For several hundred million years, the surface of the young Moon was churned up by an immense bombardment of debris that had been left over from the formation of the solar system. After this, dark lava flowed out from inside the Moon for a billion years or more, filling up the lowlands. Apart from the occasional meteorite that has dug out a new crater, the Moon has scarcely changed for the past 3,000 million years.

Large crater on the Moon's far side, photographed by the Apollo 11 astronauts while in orbit around the Moon. Inset: A lunar rock brought back to Earth by Apollo 16.

ECLIPSES

IN THE SHADE

Gradually the sky gets darker, although it is the middle of the day. Bit by bit, the Sun is going out. Birds and other animals start to bed down for the night, even though night is not yet due. Now only a thin crescent of sunlight is left. A dark shadow sweeps over the land as the last remaining chinks of sunlight are extinguished. The Sun has been totally eclipsed.

A total eclipse of the Sun is the most stunning spectacle of nature. Not surprisingly, ancient people were terrified by eclipses, for they thought that the Sun might vanish forever. One Chinese superstition was that a dragon was trying to eat the Sun. They used to bang gongs to drive the dragon away—needless to say, they always succeeded.

A solar eclipse occurs when the Moon comes between Earth and the Sun, blocking off its light. This would happen once a month, at each new Moon, were it not for the fact that the Moon's orbit is tilted, so that the Moon usually passes above or below the Sun as seen from Earth. But at least twice a year the Moon lines up with the Sun to cause a solar eclipse.

At an eclipse of the Sun, the Moon's shadow falls on part of the Earth. People inside the dark central portion of this shadow, the umbra, see the Sun fully eclipsed. As the Moon moves in its orbit, the shadow sweeps across the Earth's surface. The total eclipse lasts only a few minutes while the Moon's umbra is passing. The path of totality is only 125 miles (about 200 kilometers) wide, so that a total eclipse of the Sun is a rare sight from any given place on Earth.

During totality, a beautiful halo of faint gases known as the corona springs into view around the Sun. This is the only time that it can easily be seen and studied, which is why astronomers travel across the world to view total eclipses.

Total eclipses of the Sun occur when the Moon blots out all the bright disc of the Sun (top diagram). *The Sun's corona then becomes visible* (photo, left). *But at times, when the Moon is in the farthest part of its elliptically-shaped orbit from Earth, it appears too small to cover the Sun's disc entirely, and a ring of light remains visible even at mid-eclipse* (bottom diagram). *This is known as an annular eclipse.*

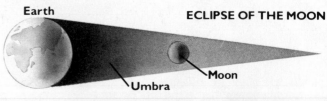

ECLIPSE OF THE MOON

Earth

Moon

Umbra

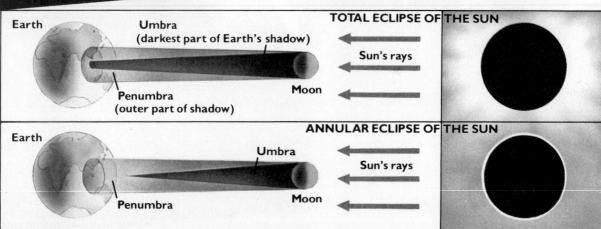

Earth

Umbra
(darkest part of Earth's shadow)

TOTAL ECLIPSE OF THE SUN

Sun's rays

Moon

Penumbra
(outer part of shadow)

Earth

Umbra

ANNULAR ECLIPSE OF THE SUN

Sun's rays

Moon

Penumbra

Moon

Outside the narrow band of totality is a much larger area of shadow known as the penumbra, inside which people see a partial eclipse of the Sun. Partial eclipses of the Sun can last for an hour or more.

ECLIPSES OF THE MOON

About twice a year the Moon enters the shadow of the Earth and an eclipse of the Moon occurs. Unlike eclipses of the Sun, which can only be seen in the limited area on which the Moon's shadow falls, an eclipse of the Moon is visible anywhere that the Moon is above the horizon.

The Earth's shadow is much larger than the Moon, and the Moon takes several hours to move through it. But even when the Moon is completely immersed in the dark central umbra of the Earth's shadow it seldom completely disappears from view. The reason is that some light reaches the Moon after being bent around the edge of the Earth by the Earth's atmosphere. Usually at a lunar eclipse the Moon turns a dark red color, but if the Earth's atmosphere contains a lot of dust or clouds then no light will get through and the Moon can then disappear in the middle of the eclipse.

WARNING

NEVER look at the Sun directly through binoculars or a telescope or you risk immediate blindness. Even staring at the Sun can damage your eyes. The only safe way to study the Sun is by projecting its image through a telescope onto a white card.

The greatest number of eclipses that can occur in any one year is seven, either five of the Sun and two of the Moon or four of the Sun and three of the Moon. Not all of these will be visible from one place on Earth.

VENUS AND MERCURY

THE HELL PLANETS

VENUS

The brightest object in the sky after the Sun and Moon is the planet Venus. It is often visible as the brilliant evening or morning "star," although it is not a star at all. Venus is a rocky body 7,500 miles (12,100 kilometers) in diameter, only slightly smaller than the Earth, wrapped in a shroud of unbroken white clouds that permanently veil its surface from telescopes on Earth.

Spacecraft sent to Venus have parachuted into its atmosphere and landed on its surface. They found that Venus fits in exactly with our idea of Hell! At the planet's surface the temperature is a furnacelike 865°F (460°C). The dense atmosphere consists of unbreathable carbon dioxide gas, which bears down with a crushing pressure 90 times that of the Earth's atmosphere. The surface is bathed in an orange gloom, pierced by constant flashes of lightning. And the all-enveloping clouds are made of corrosive sulphuric acid, stronger than that in a car's battery. So a luckless astronaut who crash-landed on Venus would be instantaneously crushed, roasted, and suffocated, and the

remains of his or her body would be eaten away by a rain of acid droplets!

Venus is odd because it spins on its axis from east to west, the opposite direction to that of the Earth and other planets which spin from west to east. Odder still, it spins very slowly, taking 243 Earth days to turn once on its axis. This is longer than the 225 days it takes to orbit the Sun. Why

Swirling clouds of Venus, as photographed by the Pioneer-Venus spacecraft orbiting the planet.

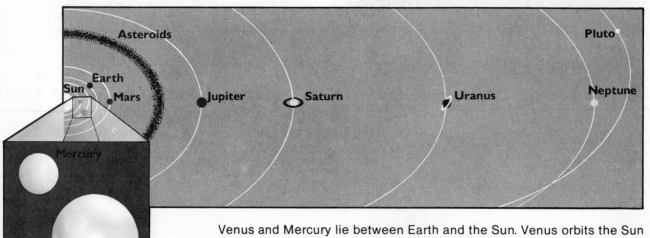

Venus and Mercury lie between Earth and the Sun. Venus orbits the Sun every 225 days at a distance of 67 million miles (108 million kilometers). It can come to within 25 million miles (40 million kilometers) of the Earth, closer than any other planet. Its closeness, and its reflective clouds, make it appear exceptionally bright. Small telescopes show that Venus goes through phases like those of the Moon as it orbits the Sun. Mercury is much more difficult to observe because of its proximity to the Sun.

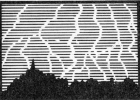

Venus has such a slow back-to-front rotation remains a puzzle.

Spacecraft have used radar to map the surface of Venus, for radar beams can penetrate the planet's clouds. Venus is a world of rolling plains interspread with highlands apparently formed by volcanic action. Some of the volcanoes may still be erupting today. In the northern hemisphere of Venus is a "continent" bigger than the United States with mountains that tower 7.5 miles (12 kilometers) above the planet's average surface level, higher than Mount Everest on Earth. Along the equator is an even larger continent, half the size of Africa, cut by rift valleys.

MERCURY

Venus is not the closest planet to the Sun. That distinction belongs to the planet Mercury, which orbits the Sun every 88 days at an average distance of 36 million miles (58 million kilometers). Mercury is 3,000 miles (4,900 kilometers) in diameter, only one and a half times larger than our own Moon, and like the Moon it is airless and waterless. Mercury also looks very much like the Moon, being peppered with craters of all sizes formed by the impact of meteorites. The sunlit side of Mercury is blasted by lethal doses of solar radiation. Temperatures there reach over 750°F (400°C), hot enough to melt tin and lead, while on the night side of Mercury temperatures fall to −274°F (−170°C). Because it is so close to the Sun, Mercury is hard to see.

Left: *A sharp, young crater about 7 miles (12 kilometers) wide within an older, eroded crater on Mercury.* Below: *A curving cliff over 200 miles (300 kilometers) long on Mercury photographed by the Mariner 10 probe.*

MARS

LIFE ON THE RED PLANET?

In 1976 two American space probes called Viking landed on the surface of the planet Mars to search for life. From the surface of Mars the probes relayed back to Earth spectacular photographs showing that the planet is covered by red deserts strewn with rocks of all sizes. Even the sky on Mars is pink, caused by fine dust in the atmosphere. But there was no sign of any plants or animals.

Under the control of their on-board computers, the Viking probes reached out robot arms to scoop up handfuls of Mars' soil. These samples were carefully examined by the equipment aboard the Vikings in the hope of finding evidence of microscopic life forms. But nothing living was found in the soil. Scientists were reluctantly forced to conclude that there is no life on Mars.

This negative result is not too surprising in view of other findings about Mars. Its air is as thin as the air 22 miles (35 kilometers) above the Earth, and its maximum daytime temperature is −20°F (−29°C), dropping lower at night. Mars is a world locked in an ice age.

Mars, though, has a fascinating landscape which includes the largest known volcano in the solar system, Olympus Mons. With a diameter of 370 miles (600 kilometers) and a height of 16 miles (26 kilometers), Olympus Mons is larger even than the volcanic islands of Hawaii on Earth. Mars also has what appear to be dried-up river channels. Evidently there was once liquid water on the surface of the planet. But Mars is too cold, and its atmosphere is too thin, for liquid water to exist there today, although the polar caps contain ice. Most remarkable of all is an immense rift valley (caused by faults in the planet's surface) 2,500 miles (4,000 kilometers) long, enough to span the United States.

Seen through a telescope from Earth, Mars appears as an orange-colored ball with dusky markings.

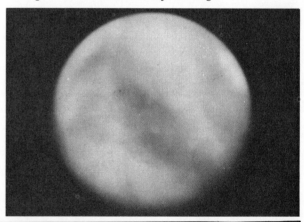

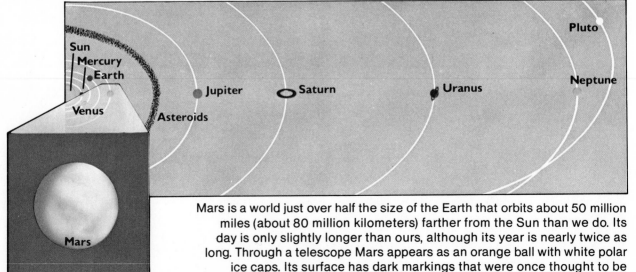

Mars is a world just over half the size of the Earth that orbits about 50 million miles (about 80 million kilometers) farther from the Sun than we do. Its day is only slightly longer than ours, although its year is nearly twice as long. Through a telescope Mars appears as an orange ball with white polar ice caps. Its surface has dark markings that were once thought to be vegetation but which are now known to be expanses of rock and dust.

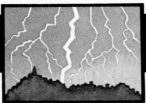

Left: *Phobos, the larger of the two moons of Mars, photographed by the Viking I space probe.*
Above: *The red sands and pink skies of Mars seen from the Viking I lander probe. Part of the craft appears in the foreground.*

THE MOONS OF MARS

Mars has two moons, called Phobos and Deimos. They are both small, cratered chunks of rock shaped like lumpy potatoes, with maximum diameters of 17 and 9 miles (27 and 15 kilometers) respectively. Phobos and Deimos are probably both former asteroids that have been captured by the gravitational pull of Mars. The asteroids are a swarm of thousands of small bodies that orbit in a belt between Mars and Jupiter.

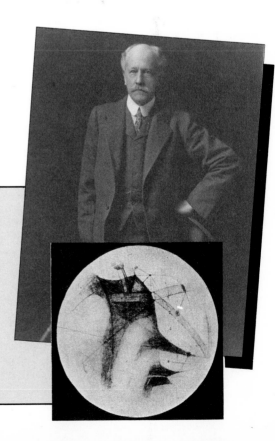

The canals of Mars

An American astronomer named Percival Lowell (right) popularized the idea that there might be life on Mars. In the early years of this century he observed what he thought was a network of canals on Mars. Lowell presumed that these had been built by a Martian civilization to bring water from the planet's polar caps to their crops on the deserts of Mars. Lowell wrote books about his theory of life on Mars. But other astronomers failed to see the canals, and space probes have finally confirmed that they do not exist. Lowell was the victim of an optical illusion. On the right is his map of Mars and the canals.

SATURN

THE RINGED PLANET

One of the most beautiful objects in the heavens is Saturn, the ringed planet. Through a telescope, Saturn appears as an ochre-colored ball whose rings girdle its equator like a flat disc. Saturn is a giant planet, nine times the diameter of the Earth. It is very different in nature from the Earth, consisting of a rocky center covered by a deep ocean of liquid hydrogen, and topped by dense clouds. The rings are made of billions of frozen lumps of ice and rock, orbiting the planet like a swarm of snowballs.

As seen from the distance of Earth, the rings have three main sections. The central part, called Ring B, is the brightest. It is separated from the outer Ring A by a 2,000-mile (3,000-kilometer) gap known as Cassini's Division. Between Ring B and the planet's cloud tops lies the transparent Ring C, also known as the Crepe Ring. But in close-up the rings turn out to be far more complex, as revealed when the Voyager space probes reached Saturn in 1980 and 1981.

The Voyager photographs showed that the rings of Saturn consist of thousands of narrow ringlets, looking like the ridges and grooves of a gramophone record. Even Cassini's Division contained slender ringlets. Beyond the outer edge of the rings is a newly discovered ring, Ring F, that consists of twisted strands like a rope. In places, particles of fine dust overlay the rings to form dark patches termed spokes.

One incredible fact about the rings of Saturn is how they are. From rim to rim, the rings span 170,000 miles (275,000 kilometers). Yet they are no more than 300 feet (100 meters) from top to bottom. If the thickness of this page represented the thickness of Saturn's rings, it would have to be 1,000 feet (300 meters) across to represent the width of the rings. The rings are probably the building blocks of a moon that never formed.

THE MOONS OF SATURN

Saturn has at least 20 moons, more than any other planet in the solar system. Many of them are insignificant lumps of rock, but the largest, Titan, is bigger than the planet Mercury. Titan is the only moon in the Solar System to possess a substantial atmosphere. This atmosphere is topped with a smoggy layer that blankets Titan's surface from view. Astronomers think that a rain of methane droplets may fall from the smoggy skies of Titan into methane seas on the moon's surface.

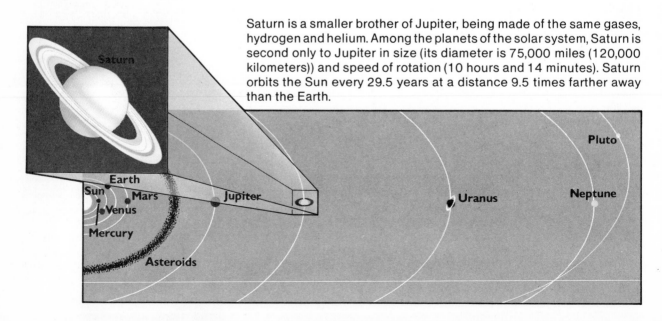

Saturn is a smaller brother of Jupiter, being made of the same gases, hydrogen and helium. Among the planets of the solar system, Saturn is second only to Jupiter in size (its diameter is 75,000 miles (120,000 kilometers)) and speed of rotation (10 hours and 14 minutes). Saturn orbits the Sun every 29.5 years at a distance 9.5 times farther away than the Earth.

 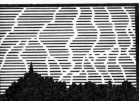  

One startling picture from the Voyager probes showed that the moon Mimas, a mere 250 miles (400 kilometers) in diameter, is scarred by an immense crater fully one-third its diameter. The impact that caused this crater must almost have shattered Mimas.

Right: *Huge craters on Saturn's moon Mimas.*
Below: *Close-up of the complex rings of Saturn.*
Bottom: *Craters and ridges on the moon Enceladus.*

Although Saturn is so large, the material of which it is made is not very densely packed. Saturn is unique among the planets in that its average density is less than that of water. Therefore, given a large ocean, Saturn would float on it.

JUPITER

A GIANT LIQUID BALL

Jupiter is the giant planet of the solar system. It is 11 times the diameter of the Earth and weighs two and a half times as much as all the other planets rolled together. But Jupiter is not solid. It is an immense ball of liquid hydrogen, wrapped in a swirling layer of multi-colored clouds. We could never land on Jupiter. If a space probe parachuted into the planet's atmosphere, as the American craft called Galileo is due to do in 1988, it would continue to fall until it was crushed by the atmospheric pressure, and its flattened remains would eventually splash into the sluggish liquid interior of Jupiter 600 miles (1,000 kilometers) below the cloud tops.

Jupiter's rapid rotation of under 10 hours, the fastest of any planet, forces the clouds into parallel bands. Traces of various chemicals in the planet's atmosphere color the clouds red, brown, yellow and sometimes even blue. Among the ever-changing weather patterns on Jupiter, one feature has stood out through telescopes on Earth for over 300 years: the Great Red Spot, the biggest and longest-lasting storm in the solar system.

The Great Red Spot is 8,700 miles (14,000 kilometers) wide and 25,000 miles (40,000 kilo-meters) long, enough to swallow a row of three Earths. It is a spinning storm cloud like an enormous hurricane, fed by currents of warm air rising from Jupiter's interior. The top of the Red Spot is the highest point on Jupiter, five miles (eight kilometers) above the level of the surrounding cloud deck. Red phosphorus, or perhaps sulphur, welling up from deep within Jupiter's atmosphere is thought to account for the distinctive color of the Great Red Spot.

JUPITER'S HOT MOON IO

Jupiter has at least 16 moons, the four largest of which were discovered in 1610 by Galileo. These four main moons are bright enough to be seen through binoculars, but before the Voyager space probes got to Jupiter in 1979 no one could have guessed that one of them, Io, was the most volcanically active body in the solar system.

On the Voyager photographs Io appears as a blotchy disc resembling a rotting orange. Voyager's cameras photographed eight volcanoes erupting simultaneously on Io. In all, this strange world, slightly larger than our own Moon, is mottled with hundreds of volcanic vents which

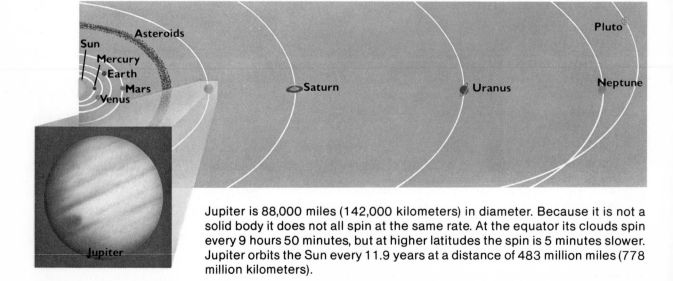

Jupiter is 88,000 miles (142,000 kilometers) in diameter. Because it is not a solid body it does not all spin at the same rate. At the equator its clouds spin every 9 hours 50 minutes, but at higher latitudes the spin is 5 minutes slower. Jupiter orbits the Sun every 11.9 years at a distance of 483 million miles (778 million kilometers).

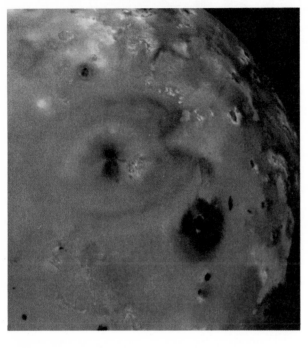

Above: *Jupiter's swirling Red Spot, photographed by Voyager. Note also a large white cloud below it.*
Left: *The fantastic surface of Jupiter's volcanic moon Io, seen from the Voyager 1 space probe.*

show up as black spots. Unlike the volcanoes on Earth, these vents do not sit at the top of mountains, but open directly onto the surface.

Io's volcanoes erupt, not lava, but molten sulphur, which gives the surface its weird colors. Where hottest, in the volcanic vents themselves, the sulphur appears black. Where the sulphur has flowed onto the surface and cooled it has turned red, orange and yellow. Each year enough sulphur to cover the whole of the surface of Io to a depth of as much as 0.4 inches (one centimeter) is erupted from the interior. Io is a world that is literally turning itself inside out.

Two sources are thought to account for Io's heat. Firstly, it is continually stretched and squeezed by the opposing gravitational pulls of Jupiter and the moons of Europa and Ganymede.

This gravitational tug-of-war produces enough friction within Io to melt its interior. Secondly, as Io moves through the intense magnetic field of Jupiter, electrical currents are set up across it that heat it like an electric fire.

Composite photograph of Jupiter with its four largest moons: orange Io, icy Europa, blotchy Ganymede and (right foreground) part of Callisto. Ganymede, Callisto and Io are larger than our own Moon: Europa is only slightly smaller. They are known as the Galilean satellites because they were discovered by Galileo. All four are bright enough to be visible in binoculars. Note also the Great Red Spot in Jupiter's southern hemisphere.

URANUS, NEPTUNE AND PLUTO

OUT OF SIGHT OF THE NAKED EYE

URANUS

On the night of March 13, 1781, an astronomer named William Herschel, observing through his telescope from the back garden of his home in Bath, England, noticed an object with a rounded disc that moved its position over the next few nights, proving that it was in orbit around the Sun. William Herschel had discovered a new planet. The new planet, named Uranus, was the first ever to be found with a telescope—the planets from Mercury to Saturn are bright enough to be seen with the naked eye and had been known since ancient times.

Uranus is 32,000 miles (51,800 kilometers) in diameter, four times as big as the Earth, and orbits the Sun every 84 years at a distance of nearly 1,800 million miles (3,000 million kilometers). Through a telescope Uranus appears as a greenish, featureless disc. The greenish color is caused by methane in its atmosphere.

One remarkable fact about Uranus is that its axis of rotation is tilted at over 90 degrees to the upright, as though the planet had been knocked on its side by some collision. As a result of this extreme tilt, one pole of Uranus experiences 42 years of daylight, followed by 42 years of darkness as the planet moves on its orbit around the Sun.

Uranus has five known moons and a set of nine faint rings around its equator.

NEPTUNE

As astronomers followed the movement of Uranus, it became clear that the planet was not moving along its orbit as expected. Some astronomers suspected that it was being pulled out of position by the gravity of another, as yet unknown planet. Quite independently John Couch Adams in England and Urbain Leverrier in France calculated where the disturbing planet

Above: *William Herschel, discoverer of Uranus, holds a diagram of the planet and two of its satellites.* Right: *Artist's impression of Uranus and its narrow rings.*

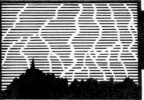

might lie, and on September 23, 1846, the planet Neptune was found close to the position they had predicted.

Neptune is a near-twin of Uranus, being a mere 1,250 miles (2,000 kilometers) smaller. Neptune orbits the Sun every 165 years at a distance of 2,800 million miles (4,500 million kilometers). It has two moons, the larger of which, Triton, is 1,900 miles (over 3,000 kilometers) in diameter. Triton is gradually spiralling closer to Neptune, and will eventually break up to form a set of rings around the planet.

PLUTO

After the discovery of Neptune, astronomers began to wonder if another planet might exist undiscovered at the edge of the Solar System. But it was not until 1930 that the ninth planet, Pluto, was finally discovered, as a result of a round-the-sky photographic search by Clyde Tombaugh at the Lowell Observatory in Arizona.

Pluto turned out to be a strange body indeed. Its 250-year orbit around the Sun crosses that of Neptune, so that from January 1979 until March 1999 Pluto actually lies closer to the Sun than Neptune. Its average distance from the Sun is 3,600 million miles (5,900 million kilometers). Pluto is the smallest planet in the solar system, with a diameter of 1,900 miles (3,000 kilometers), smaller than our own Moon. In composition, Pluto is thought to consist mostly of frozen ice, like a gigantic snowball.

Pluto has one moon, called Charon, nearly half the planet's diameter. Charon orbits Pluto in 6 days 9 hours, the same time that the planet takes to spin on its axis. So Charon hangs permanently fixed over one point on Pluto.

Artist's impressions of Neptune and its largest moon Triton (above), *and Pluto and Charon* (below).

Clyde Tombaugh pictured on the 50th anniversary of his discovery of Pluto.

A tenth planet?

Does a tenth planet lurk undiscovered in the darkness of space beyond Pluto? Astronomers have looked for such an object, but they have never found it. Such an object, if it exists, would have to be either very small or very distant to have escaped detection. Probably there are no more planets beyond Pluto.

THE SUN

A HUGE NUCLEAR REACTOR

Thousands of stars are visible at night, but during the day we see just one star: the Sun. We rely on it for all the heat and light that keeps us alive. Our Sun is an average star, an incandescent ball of gas 865,000 miles (1.4 million kilometers) in diameter, 109 times wider than the Earth. It appears bigger and brighter than the night-time stars simply because it is so much closer to us. If we could travel to the other stars, we would find that they look like the Sun.

The Sun consists mostly of hydrogen gas, the most plentiful substance in the Universe. The visible surface of the Sun, known as the photosphere, is not solid; rather it is a seething mass of gas, whose temperature is 10,800°F (6,000°C). At the center of the Sun, the temperature rises to an astounding 27 million°F (15 million°C).

The photosphere is marked by a number of dark blotches called sunspots. Also, flames of hot gas called prominences leap millions of kilometers into space from the edge of the Sun. Prominences can be seen either with special instruments, or at eclipses of the Sun when the Moon blots out the light from the photosphere.

The Sun's crowning glory is a halo of faint gas

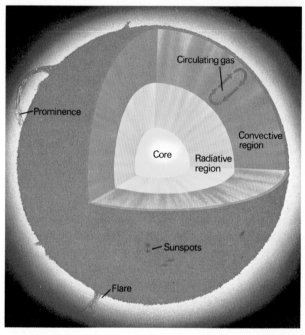

Cutaway of the Sun. Energy is produced in the core and flows outward, completing its journey to the surface in vast circulating cells of hot gas.

called the corona, which is seen shining with a pearly glow around the Sun at total eclipses.

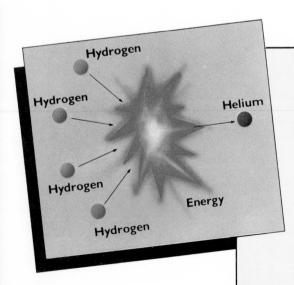

What makes the Sun shine?

The center of the Sun is like a giant nuclear reactor. There, atoms of hydrogen gas are crushed together to make atoms of helium, which is slightly heavier. In the process, energy is given off, and the energy produced in the reaction is what keeps the Sun shining. All other stars shine by the same processes. Every second, 600 million tons of hydrogen are turned into helium inside the Sun. But the sun contains enough hydrogen to keep shining for billions of years.

How far is the Sun?

The Sun is 93 million miles (150 million kilometers) away from us. Light takes eight minutes 19 seconds to cross this distance. Therefore, if the sun were to go out at this instant, we would not notice for over eight minutes.

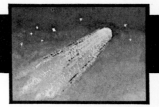

The corona consists of gas boiled off from the Sun's surface. Gas from the corona streams away from the Sun, forming the so-called "solar wind" that flows past the Earth and other planets. Therefore we can be said to lie within the tenuous outer reaches of the Sun's corona.

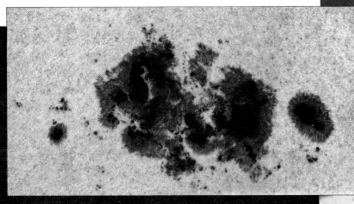

Cooler gas on the Sun's surface forms dark sunspots, such as this group many times larger than the Earth.

SUNSPOTS

Dark markings called sunspots come and go on the Sun's surface. They are areas of cooler gas. Even a small sunspot is about the size of the Earth, but the largest ones form into groups that can extend for 60,000 miles (100,000 kilometers) or more. A typical sunspot lasts for a week or two before dying away. The number of sunspots rises to a peak every 11 years or so, when 100 or more spots can be visible at a time. At times of minimum sunspot activity, no spots may be seen for days on end. Sometimes, brilliant eruptions called flares burst out on the Sun's surface near

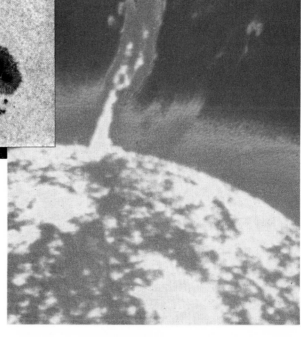

Hot gases leap into space from the edge of the Sun, as seen by telescopes on the Skylab space station.

sunspots. These flares eject atomic particles into space which cause aurorae (see page 18). Such storms on the Sun's surface are thought to affect weather on Earth.

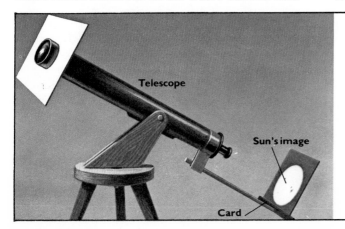
Telescope
Sun's image
Card

WARNING

NEVER look at the Sun directly through binoculars or a telescope or you risk immediate blindness. Even staring at the Sun can damage your eyes. The only safe way to study the sun is by projecting its image through a telescope onto a white card.

OTHER PLANETARY SYSTEMS

SYSTEMS

THE SEARCH FOR WOBBLING STARS

Are there planets around other stars? Astronomers think it unlikely that our Sun should be the only star to have a family of planets. But any planets around other stars would be too faint to see through telescopes on Earth, so astronomers have had to resort to indirect methods of detection. Their exciting results show that other planetary systems may be quite common.

The biggest breakthrough has come from the Infrared Astronomy Satellite, IRAS, which observed the sky at infrared wavelengths during 1983 (the infrared part of the spectrum lies between visible light and radio waves). IRAS detected signs of planetary systems being formed around several stars, notably Vega, the fifth brightest star in the sky. IRAS found that Vega is ringed by a cloud of cold gas and dust containing particles that range in size from pebbles to chunks several kilometers across. Our own solar system is believed to have formed from such a

disc of matter around the Sun 4,600 million years ago. The disc around Vega has a mass about the same as all the planets around our Sun, and its diameter is twice that of the orbit of the planet Neptune. There could be full-sized planets around Vega, but IRAS could not see clearly enough to distinguish them.

Astronomers using specially sensitive detectors have photographed a disc of dust and gas that IRAS found around another star, Beta Pictoris. Planets may exist unseen in the inner part of this disc, close to the star itself. Here we

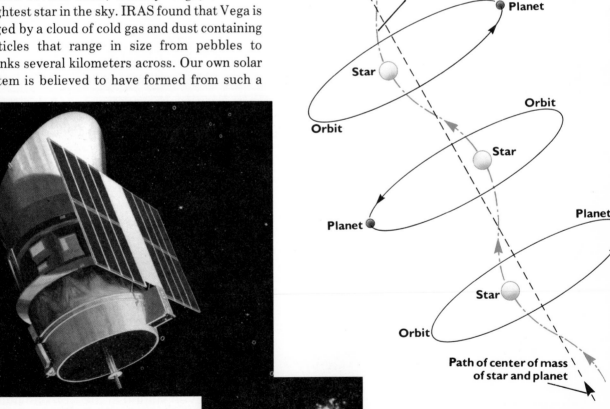

Above: *The snaking movement of a star through space reveals the existence of companion planets. A star and a planet are like the unequal ends of a dumbbell. As the planet moves around its orbit, the star wobbles from side to side.*

Above: *IRAS, the Infrared Astronomy Satellite, found evidence of planetary systems around stars.*
Right: *A disc of matter, probably a forming planetary system, photographed around the star Beta Pictoris.*

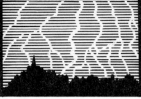

have direct visual evidence of the birth of a planetary system around a star.

Another way of searching for planets is to look for the slight wobble they cause in the motion of their parent star. An American astronomer, Peter van de Kamp, has announced the existence of a wobble of the nearby Barnard's Star. He calculates that the wobble is due to two planets similar to Jupiter and Saturn in orbit around Barnard's Star. Astronomers are now studying other stars for the tell-tale wobbles produced by planets around them.

FORMATION OF THE SOLAR SYSTEM

Large cloud of gas and dust in space starts to collapse

Central star is formed, surrounded by a doughnut-shaped ring of material

Collisions between particles build up solid lumps of matter and the disc starts to thin out

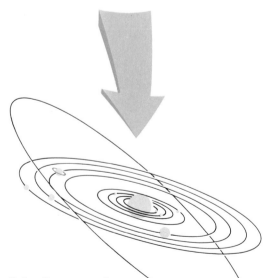

The Solar System today

HOW PLANETS FORM

When our Sun was born 4,600 million years ago, it was surrounded by a disc of dust and gas. In the part of the disc nearest the Sun, the dust specks collided and stuck together, building themselves up into larger lumps that eventually combined to form the planets Mercury, Venus, Earth and Mars. In the cold outer regions of the solar system, the ring broke up into large blobs of gas which gave rise to the giant planets Jupiter, Saturn, Uranus and Neptune. The remaining gas was blown out of the solar system by the Sun. The whole process of the formation of the planets took about 100 million years. Astronomers now think that the formation of planets is a natural by-product of the birth of stars, so that other stars may have a solar system similar to our own.

Stars and Planets

The difference between a star and a planet is that stars give out their own heat and light, while planets are cold bodies that shine by reflecting sunlight.

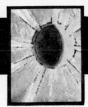

BIRTHPLACES OF THE STARS

CLOUDS OF GAS

Fifteen hundred light years away from Earth lies one of the most entrancing objects in the heavens: the Orion Nebula, a wispy mass of gas and dust in which stars are being born. It is visible to the naked eye as a misty patch in the constellation of Orion, but on long-exposure photographs through telescopes it takes on the appearance of some exotic tropical flower. At the center of the Nebula are four stars recently spawned from the surrounding gas. The light of these stars makes the Nebula glow. Astronomers estimate that the Orion Nebula contains enough gas to produce thousands more stars. This is a veritable star factory.

Our own Sun and planets were born from such a cloud of gas 4,600 million years ago. A star forms when a small knot of gas, denser than the surrounding nebula, begins to shrink under the inward pull of its gravity. As the knot of gas gets smaller and denser it heats up. Finally, at the center of the gas ball, the conditions of temperature and density become so great that nuclear reactions start, releasing energy that turns the gas blob into a self-luminous star. Those nuclear reactions keep the star burning for the rest of its life. From the time that a star like the Sun begins contracting to the moment that its nuclear reactions switch on takes about 10 million years.

Although the Orion Nebula is the most celebrated, it is far from being the only gas cloud in space. Many others are scattered throughout the spiral arms of our Galaxy. The photographs on these pages show some of the most beautiful.

HOW LONG DO STARS LIVE?

The lifetime of a star depends on its mass. Surprisingly, the heaviest stars burn out the most quickly, whereas the lightest stars live the longest because they burn their fuel more slowly. A star with 10 times the mass of the Sun burns up all its fuel and dies in 100 million years, only one hundredth of the Sun's lifetime. On the other hand, a star with one-tenth the mass of the Sun can last for a trillion years. The Sun is estimated to be about halfway through its 10,000 million year lifetime.

Right: *The beautiful Orion Nebula is a birthplace of stars. Its central regions are shown in detail at left. Inset right: The colorful Trifid Nebula.*

Nebula is a Latin word meaning mist. The plural is nebulae. Nebulae are extremely insubstantial. Even the densest of them is far thinner than the gas of our atmosphere. On the left are the four stars at the center of the Orion Nebula, known as the Trapezium, and (inset) the North American Nebula in Cygnus, so called because of its shape.

 # OTHER SUNS

STARS BIG AND SMALL

In the night sky, stars appear as points of light. Yet in reality they are glowing balls of gas similar in nature to the Sun, only very much farther away. By careful study of the stars' light, astronomers have found that stars come in a wide range of sizes and brightnesses, from tiny dwarfs a fraction the size of the Sun, to immense giants hundreds of times bigger than the Sun.

The largest stars are the red supergiants, such as Antares in the constellation of Scorpius, and Betelgeuse in the constellation of Orion. Such stars have diameters about 300 times that of our Sun. If either Antares or Betelgeuse were placed where our Sun now is, the orbit of the Earth would lie underneath their surfaces. Antares and Betelgeuse are both so large that they are unstable. They expand and contract, getting slightly brighter and fainter as they do so.

At the other end of the scale are the dwarfs, stars much smaller than the Sun. The second-closest star to the Sun, called Barnard's Star, is a red dwarf that, if our Sun were such a star, we on Earth would freeze.

Smaller still are the white dwarfs. These are the shrunken remains of ordinary stars, such as the Sun, which have run out of energy at the end of their lives. A white dwarf is only about one hundredth the diameter of our Sun, that is similar in size to the Earth. Yet as much matter as is in the entire sun can be squeezed into that small ball. Consequently white dwarfs are extremely dense, far denser than any substance known on Earth. A spoonful of material from a white dwarf would weigh several tons.

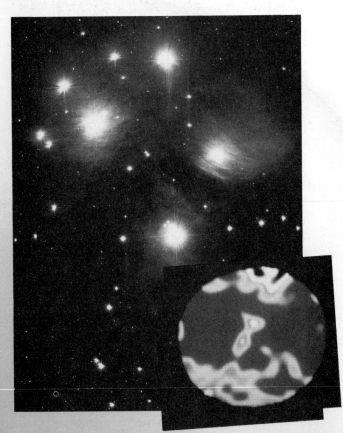

SUN

Far left: *The Pleiades in the constellation of Taurus. Some stars group together in families. The Pleiades is a family of blue giant stars that have been born within the past few million years, which, on the celestial time scale, makes them very young.*

Left: *The face of the red supergiant star Betelgeuse, photographed at Kitt Peak Observatory, Arizona.*

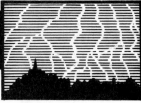

HOW FAR ARE THE STARS?

Astronomers measure distances to the stars in light years, which is the distance traveled by a beam of light in one year. A light year is equivalent to 5.9 trillion miles (9.5 trillion kilometers). Even the nearest star to the Sun, Alpha Centauri, is over four light years away, which means that light from it has taken more than four years to get here. Many of the stars in the night sky are hundreds or even thousands of light years away, so the light that we are now receiving from them left those stars centuries ago.

ALPHA CENTAURI

160,000 YEARS

The Space Shuttle traveling at top speed, would take 160,000 years to reach the nearest star to the Sun, Alpha Centauri.

COMPARATIVE SIZES OF VARIOUS STARS

Antares, red supergiant

Rigel, blue-white

Barnard's Star, red dwarf

Sirius A, white

Sun, yellow-white

Sirius B, white dwarf

Star colors

At first sight all stars appear white, but close examination shows that they come in a range of colors from red to blue. The color of a star tells us its temperature. The reddest stars are the coolest, with surface temperatures down to 5,400°F (3,000°C). The bluest stars are the hottest, with temperatures of 45,000°F (25,000°C) or more. The Sun is a yellow-white star, average in both temperature and size.

Why do stars twinkle?

Stars appear to twinkle, but this is nothing to do with the stars themselves. The twinkling effect is caused by movements in the Earth's atmosphere.

STARDEATH

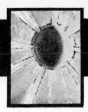

SUPERNOVAE, RED GIANTS AND WHITE DWARFS

From time to time in the depths of space, a star explodes in a blaze of glory. In such an eruption, termed a supernova, we witness the death of a massive star. A supernova can temporarily shine as brightly as billions of stars like the Sun. Then, after a few months, the dying star fades back into obscurity, leaving only a few faint strands of twisted wreckage to mark the site of its self-destruction.

To become a supernova, a star must have a mass at least 10 times greater than that of the Sun. Toward the end of its life, such a heavyweight star undergoes a runaway series of nuclear reactions at its center, finally becoming unstable and blowing up. In a supernova's inferno, all the chemical elements of nature are produced and are scattered into space, eventually to be collected up into new stars, and perhaps new planets and life. The atoms of which we and the Earth are made were produced inside the nuclear reactors of ancient supernovae.

A supernova does not always destroy the entire star. In some cases, the central core of the star remains after the explosion, tightly compressed into either a neutron star or a black hole.

Supernovae are plentiful in other galaxies, but the last supernova seen in our own Galaxy was in 1604. Another one is long overdue, and could occur at any time. When it does, it will be a dazzling object, outshining every star in the night sky and perhaps even casting shadows.

THE CRAB NEBULA

In AD 1054, astronomers in China saw a brilliant new star flare up in the constellation Taurus, the Bull. It shone so brightly that it was visible in daylight for three weeks, finally fading from naked-eye view more than a year after it first appeared. The Oriental astronomers had been watching a supernova explosion. The shattered remains of the star that exploded are visible in telescopes as a fuzzy patch known as the Crab Nebula (below) because it appeared crablike in shape to early observers.

Right: *Glowing strands of gas in the constellation Vela are the shattered remains of a star that exploded as a supernova in ancient times.*

Below: *The Crab Nebula.*

DEATH OF THE SUN

Our Sun will not die in such a violent fashion as a supernova. As it nears the end of its existence in a few thousand million years from now, it will start to swell up into a red giant, making the climate of Earth too warm for any form of life. At its largest, the red giant Sun will become as much as 100 times its present size, engulfing the orbits of Mercury and Venus and perhaps also that of the Earth. By then, the oceans and atmosphere of Earth will have boiled away.

Gradually, the outer layers of the distended red giant Sun will drift off into space, forming a gigantic smoke ring around the Sun. Stripped bare of its surrounding layers, the core of the Sun will become visible at the center of the smoke ring as a tiny, dense white dwarf star. Over billions of years this white dwarf will slowly cool to invisibility.

Right: *The Ring Nebula in Lyra is a celestial smoke ring, puffed off by a star like the Sun as it dies.*

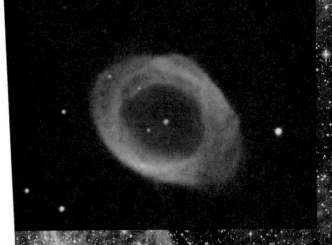

BLACK HOLES

COSMIC VACUUM CLEANERS

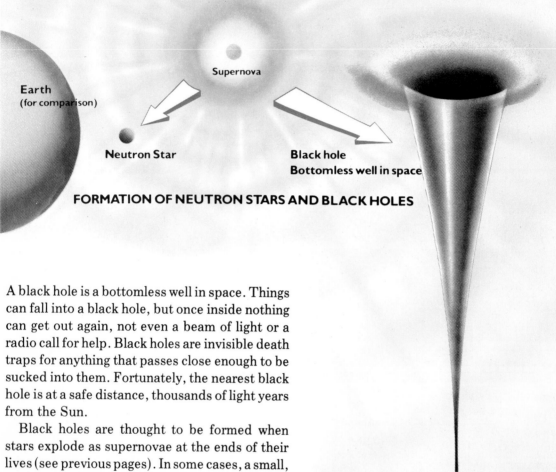

Earth
(for comparison)

Supernova

Neutron Star

Black hole
Bottomless well in space

FORMATION OF NEUTRON STARS AND BLACK HOLES

A black hole is a bottomless well in space. Things can fall into a black hole, but once inside nothing can get out again, not even a beam of light or a radio call for help. Black holes are invisible death traps for anything that passes close enough to be sucked into them. Fortunately, the nearest black hole is at a safe distance, thousands of light years from the Sun.

Black holes are thought to be formed when stars explode as supernovae at the ends of their lives (see previous pages). In some cases, a small, superdense neutron star is left behind by the explosion. But if the neutron star has a mass of more than three Suns, the inward pull of its own gravity is so great that nothing can prevent it from shrinking into a black hole.

What happens is that, as the star shrinks smaller and smaller until even the star's light is prevented from escaping. The star has become invisible. That in itself is remarkable enough, but what happens next seems to defy credibility. Since, by this stage, nothing can stop the inward force of its own gravity, the star continues to shrink until it ends up being crushed to a single point of infinitely high density. In effect, the star has shrunk itself out of existence! Yet the star's intense gravitational field remains, forming a hole in space that is ready to swallow up passing objects like a cosmic vacuum cleaner.

The size of the black hole depends on the mass of the star within it. For a star three times the mass of the Sun the diameter of the black hole is about 11 miles (18 kilometers), but is larger for greater masses. Anything that falls into the bottomless gravitational pit of the black hole will end up, like the star, being crushed out of existence.

Black holes are undoubtedly the most bizarre objects that the Universe has to offer. But since they are black, how can we detect them? Fortunately, black holes give themselves away when they suck in gas from nearby stars. As the gas swirls around the cosmic drainplug, it heats up to millions of degrees, so hot that it emits X rays. These X-ray emissions can be detected by satellites orbiting the Earth.

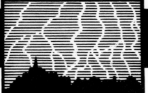

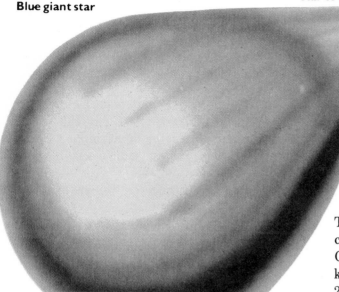

Blue giant star

Gas flows from blue giant star to black hole

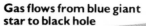

Black hole

THE BLACK HOLE IN CYGNUS

The first black hole to be discovered lies in the constellation of Cygnus, the swan. It is named Cygnus X-1, and it orbits around a blue star known simply by its catalogue number HDE 226868. From its orbit, astronomers calculate that the black hole has a mass about eight times that of the Sun. The black hole itself is invisible, but hot gas falling into it from the visible companion star gives out X rays which have been picked up by satellites. Astronomers have since detected many other likely black holes by their X-ray emissions.

NEUTRON STARS AND PULSARS

Instead of a black hole, some supernova explosions leave behind a tiny, superdense neutron star, so called because the protons and electrons of its atoms have merged to form neutrons. A neutron star contains the mass of up to three Suns compressed into a ball only 12 miles (20 kilometers) in diameter (if a neutron star has a mass more than three times that of the Sun, it collapses into a black hole). Neutron stars are unimaginably dense: a spoonful of neutron star material would weigh a thousand million tons. Neutron stars can spin many times a second, and many of them give out a flash of radiation, like a lighthouse beam, as they do so. Such flashing neutron stars are also known as pulsars. Pulsars flash at many wavelengths from X rays to radio waves. One seen flashing visually is the pulsar at the center of the Crab Nebula, shown here flashing on (top) and off (bottom).

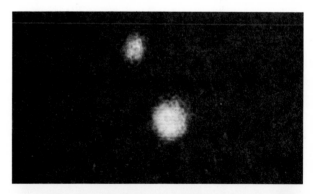

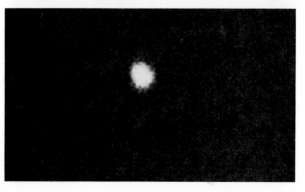

THE MILKY WAY

OUR OWN GALAXY

It is a clear, dark night. Across the sky meanders a faint stream of light called the Milky Way. The Italian astronomer Galileo Galilei turned his telescope on the Milky Way in 1610 and described it as "a mass of innumerable stars planted together in clusters." Now we know that the stars of the Milky Way are part of a spiral-shaped city of hundreds of billions of stars, spanning 100,000 light years from rim to rim. This vast stellar aggregation is known as the Galaxy.

The whole Galaxy is rotating slowly. Our Sun, which lies 30,000 light years from the center, takes about 250 million years to go around once, but other stars move at different speeds. The thickest part of the Galaxy is the central hub, which measures 12,000 light years from top to bottom. Out in the spiral arms, where we lie, the thickness of the Galaxy is reduced to about 2,000 light years.

The bright stars that we see in the night sky are among the closest to us in the Galaxy. The more distant ones mass together to form the stardust trail of the Milky Way. Our Galaxy is one of countless billions of other galaxies dotted throughout space. Its name is given a capital G to distinguish it from any other galaxy.

LEGENDS OF THE MILKY WAY

In Greek mythology, the Milky Way was a flow of milk that sprang from the breast of the goddess Juno as she suckled the infant Hercules. Norse legend regarded the Milky Way as the path of the spirits of dead heroes to Valhalla, and the North American Indians had a similar idea, as expressed in the poem *Hiawatha:* "The broad white road in heaven, pathway of the ghosts to the land of the hereafter." A legend from Finland calls it a starry bridge, built to unite two lovers in heaven. Other legends from various parts of the world have visualized the Milky Way as a heavenly river.

Above: *Dense star clouds toward the center of our Galaxy.*

Spiral arms

Plan view

Center of the Galaxy

Sun

Cross-section

THE GALAXY

GLOBULAR CLUSTERS

Gigantic, ball-shaped groups of stars swarm around our Galaxy like moths around a flame. Over 100 of these so-called globular clusters are known, the two brightest ones being visible in the southern hemisphere like two fuzzy stars, known as Omega Centauri and 47 Tucanae. Globular clusters contain anything from 10,000 stars to a million stars, packed into a ball up to 300 light years across. The stars in globular clusters are among the oldest known, with ages of more than ten thousand million years, over twice that of the Sun. Globular clusters evidently formed early in the Galaxy's history.

The globular cluster M 3.

Juno and The Infant Hercules *by the artist Tintoretto.*

Below: *The Large Magellanic Cloud, showing the Tarantula Nebula at center left.*

MAGELLANIC CLOUDS

Two faintly glowing patches of light are visible in the southern sky, like detached portions of the Milky Way. They are called the Magellanic Clouds, after the Portuguese explorer Ferdinand Magellan. They are actually small satellite galaxies to our own Galaxy. The larger of the two contains about 10 thousand million stars, roughly a tenth of the number in our own Galaxy, and lies about 180,000 light years away. Its most prominent feature is the Tarantula Nebula, a spidery-shaped cloud of gas that is the largest nebula known. If the Tarantula were as close to us as the Orion Nebula, it would appear larger than an outstretched hand and would be bright enough to cast shadows. The Small Magellanic Cloud has only about two thousand million stars, and is 200,000 light years away.

GALAXIES

STAR CITIES

Galaxies are dotted like islands throughout space as far as the largest telescopes can see. The nearest major galaxy to our own is the great spiral in Andromeda, visible to the naked eye as a hazy patch. It lies 2.2 million light years away, which means that the light we see from it today left there 2.2 million years ago when our apelike ancestors were still roaming the plains of Africa. The Andromeda galaxy is the most distant object visible to the naked eye.

The Andromeda galaxy is in many ways a twin of our own, being spiral in shape and similar in size. Spiral galaxies have beautiful curving arms of stars and gas that emerge from a central bulge of stars. Some spirals have a straight bar of stars and dust across their centers; these are termed barred spirals. Most of the galaxies visible throughout space are spirals of one kind or another, but not all. Another major class of galaxy is the elliptical galaxies, which have no spiral arms at all. The largest elliptical galaxies contain over a trillion stars, 10 times as many as our Galaxy. They are the largest congregations of stars in the Universe.

Above: *Giant elliptical galaxy M 87.*
Below: *Barred spiral galaxy NGC 1300.*

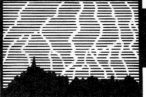

COLLIDING GALAXIES

In 1951 an astronaut at Mount Palomar Observatory in California, Walter Baade, photographed a strange, fuzzy-looking object in the constellation of Cygnus which he thought could be two galaxies in collision. A colleague challenged him to prove his conjecture, and bet him a bottle of whiskey on the outcome. Baade analyzed light from the strange object, called Cygnus A, and found that it contained much hot gas, as would be expected if two galaxies were running into each other. Baade won the bottle of whiskey.

Since then, many other examples of colliding galaxies have been found. They are the most spectacular traffic accidents in the cosmos. One peculiar object, called Centaurus A, looks like a giant elliptical galaxy with a dark ring of dust around it. Astronomers now think that this strange object results from the merger of an elliptical galaxy and a spiral galaxy.

THE QUASAR PUZZLE

Among the most baffling objects in the Universe are quasars. These objects seem to be shining with the brilliance of several normal galaxies from an area the size of our solar system. The puzzle of their immense energy and small size is not yet solved, but astronomers think that quasars are actually young galaxies with an immense black hole at their centers which rips apart passing stars and swallows their gas. On this theory, the immensely hot gas circulating around the mouth of the black hole accounts for the quasar's small, brilliant core.

Below: *Spiral galaxy M 81. Below left: The peculiar galaxy Centaurus A is crossed by a lane of dark dust. Bottom right: The Whirlpool Galaxy, a spiral with a smaller galaxy at the end of one of its arms.*

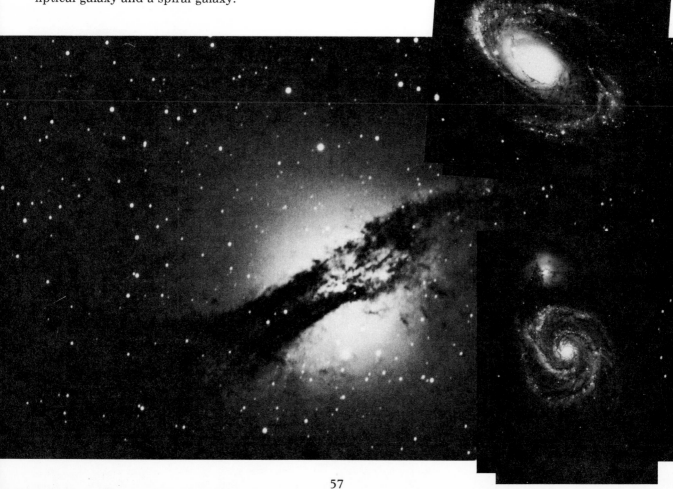

BIG BANG

THE EVER-GROWING UNIVERSE

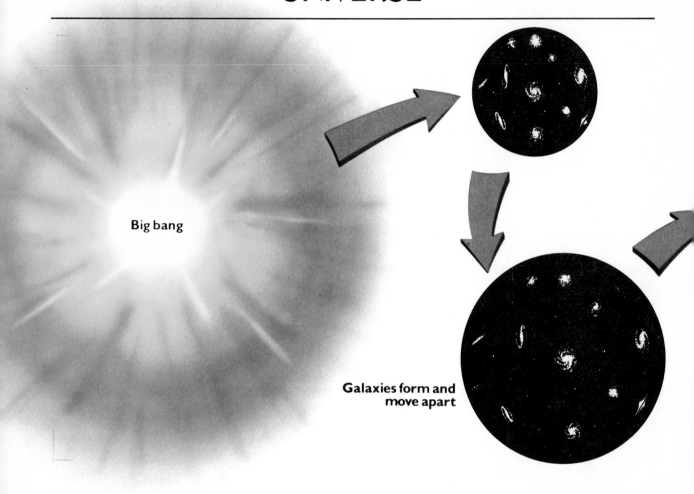

Big bang

Galaxies form and move apart

In 1929 the American astronomer Edwin Hubble made an astonishing discovery. He found that the entire Universe is expanding, like a balloon being blown up. This finding revolutionized our understanding of the Universe, and led to the modern theories of how the Universe was born.

Hubble made his discovery of the expansion of the Universe from a study of distant galaxies. All the galaxies, he found, are moving apart. And the further away a galaxy is, the faster it seems to be moving. This relationship between the distance of a galaxy in the Universe and its speed of movement is known as Hubble's Law.

If the galaxies are flying apart, then once upon a time they must all have been packed closely together. In fact, the most widely accepted theory of the origin of the Universe says that the entire Universe–all of the space and matter–once formed a superdense ball that for some unknown reason exploded. That explosion is termed the Big Bang, and it marks the origin of the Universe as we know it. Since then, all the bits from the explosion–the galaxies–have been flying outward.

By measuring the rate at which the Universe is expanding, we can work out when the Big Bang occurred. According to the best modern measurements, the galaxies are receding at a rate of about 15 miles (about 24 kilometers) per second for every million light years they are away from us. If this rate of expansion has remained the same since the origin of the Universe, then the Big Bang occurred about 15 billion years ago. Therefore the Universe is roughly three times the age of the Sun and Earth.

THE BIG BANG THEORY

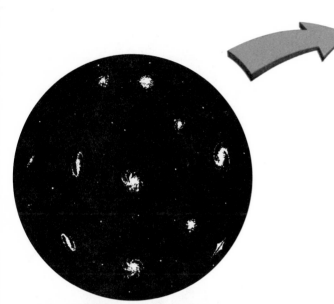

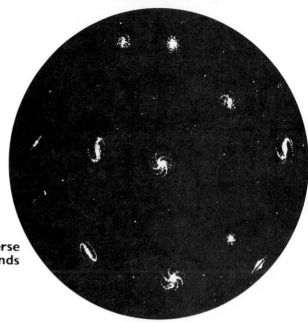

Universe expands

WILL THE UNIVERSE EXPAND FOREVER?

According to one theory, the expansion of the Universe might eventually slow down and stop. The galaxies would then fall back together again to spark off another Big Bang. According to this theory, the Universe might continue in endless cycles of expansion and contraction. However, there is no sign that the expansion of the Universe is slowing to a halt. It seems that the Universe will expand forever, thinning out as the galaxies move apart from each other. Over billions upon billions of years all the stars in those galaxies will die out and the Universe will fade into the total blackness of eternal night.

Edwin Hubble, the astronomer who discovered in 1929 that the Universe is expanding.

Two American radio engineers, Arno Penzias and Robert Wilson, heard the "echo" of the Big Bang in 1965. They were investigating radio noise on satellite transmissions when they detected a very faint hiss coming from all parts of space. This radio hiss is thought to be energy left over from the Big Bang, circulating forever in the Universe like a kind of cosmic echo. For their discovery, Penzias and Wilson, seen here with their radio telescope, were awarded the Nobel Prize in 1978.

SETI

IS ANYONE OUT THERE?

Are we alone in space? This is one of the most exciting questions being investigated by scientists. Many astronomers believe that there could be large numbers of other civilizations out there. As mentioned earlier in this book, our Sun is just one of over 100 thousand million stars in the Galaxy. About 10 percent of those stars are thought to have planets around them. If only a small fraction of those planets are like the Earth, there are still a lot of places where life may have developed.

Life on other planets would probably not look anything like life on Earth. What strange creatures might crawl, walk or fly on other worlds? Some planets will possess simple lifeforms such as grass or trees. On others, creatures like dinosaurs might reign supreme. But on some planets, highly intelligent creatures could have evolved. Astronomers estimate that as many as a million civilizations similar to, or more advanced than, our own might exist in the Galaxy.

We cannot send space probes to examine other stars, because they are too far away. But there is one way in which we could make contact with other beings in space—by radio. Radio messages flash through space at the speed of light, far faster than any spacecraft could travel. If other beings exist, they may be trying to attract our attention by beaming radio signals at us that we could pick up.

Astronomers have tried listening for incoming alien radio messages on several occasions, but without success. The National Aeronautics and Space Administration (NASA) is setting up a 10-year program called Project SETI, the search for extraterrestrial intelligence. As part of the project, scientists will use specially sensitive receivers mounted on radio telescopes to scan the entire sky in search of messages from the stars. Project SETI will last until the 1990s, by when we should know whether or not anyone out there is trying to talk to us.

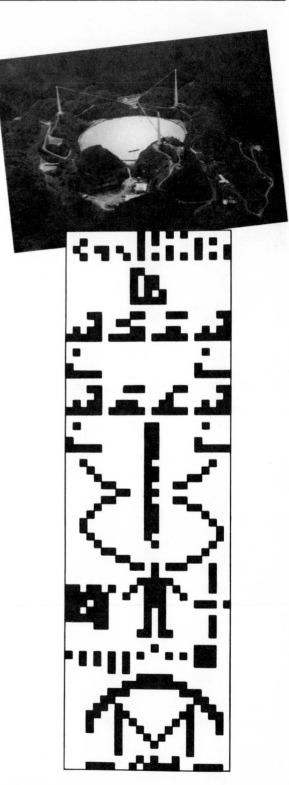

The Arecibo radio telescope (top) *and its message to other worlds* (above) *that it sent in 1974.*

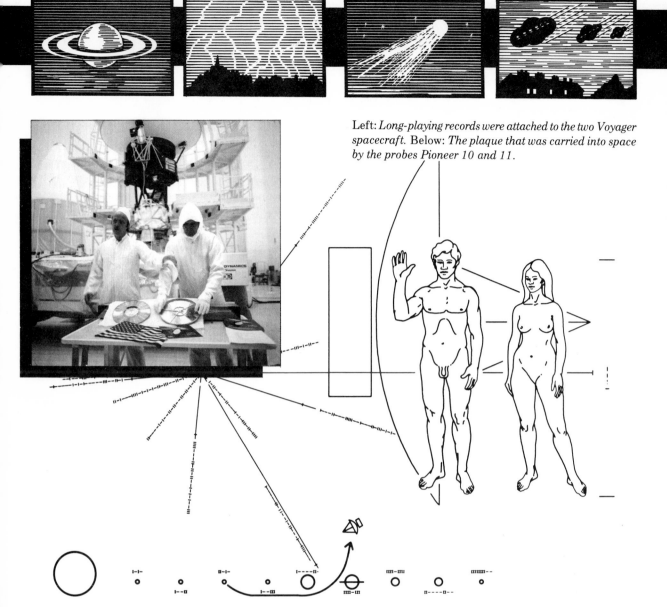

Left: *Long-playing records were attached to the two Voyager spacecraft.* Below: *The plaque that was carried into space by the probes Pioneer 10 and 11.*

THE ARECIBO MESSAGE

What would an alien radio message say? It might be sent as a form of radio pulses that could be arranged to form a picture. An example of such a message was transmitted in 1974 from the Arecibo radio telescope in Puerto Rico. This giant dish, 1,000 feet (305 meters) in diameter, is the world's largest radio telescope. The Arecibo message was beamed toward M13, a globular cluster containing 300,000 stars in the constellation Hercules. Anyone living in M13 who receives the message will be able to rearrange the radio pulses to form a simple picture. This picture tells of the chemical makeup of human bodies, what humans look like, and the planet on which we live. However, M13 is so far away that our messages will take about 25,000 years to get there.

SPACE CALLING CARDS

Four space probes, Pioneers 10 and 11 and Voyagers 1 and 2, are on course to leave the solar system, carrying messages from Earth. Any civilization that intercepts the two Pioneer probes as they fly among the stars billions of years in the future will find this simple calling card. It shows a drawing of two humans, plus directions showing where our Sun lies, and a map of our solar system. The two Voyager probes carry long-playing records. Into their grooves have been electronically encoded over 100 pictures of the Earth and its life. These are followed by spoken greetings, sounds of Earth, and a selection of music. The Voyager records and the Pioneer plaques are like cosmic messages in a bottle, cast into the sea of space. They may never be found.

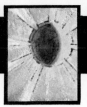

UFOS

DO THEY EXIST?

UFO is short for unidentified flying object. UFOs are popularly known as flying saucers, because that is often the shape they are reported to appear. The first flying saucers were sighted in 1947 by Kenneth Arnold, an American pilot, who reported seeing a chain of nine saucerlike objects flying in formation near Mount Rainier in Washington State. The U.S. Air Force, who investigated the sighting, put it down to a form of mirage.

Most UFOs are simply lights in the sky, usually at night. One famous example was seen by former U.S. President Jimmy Carter. He reported a brilliant UFO low in the west one evening in 1969. But when the case was investigated it was found that Carter was looking straight at the brilliant planet Venus, the most common cause of UFO reports.

Even experienced observers of the sky, such as pilots, report UFOs. In 1978 a pilot reported a flock of luminous UFOs off the coast of New Zealand. A TV cameraman went up with the pilot and filmed the UFOs. They turned out to be lights on boats fishing for squid, according to an investigation by New Zealand scientists.

In 1980, American airmen at Woodbridge air base in England reported seeing a brilliant flashing UFO in a nearby forest. Investigators who visited the site found that the airmen had been looking at a lighthouse on the coastline.

UFOs are also reported on radar. But birds, insects and atmospheric effects can all cause false radar images that might be mistaken for UFOs.

Most bizarre are the reports that tell of close encounters with landed spacecraft and aliens aboard them. But there is never any independent evidence to back up these stories. George Adamski, an American, claimed in 1954 to have met beings from Venus, Mars and Saturn and to have been given rides aboard their flying saucers. In 1975, an American forestry worker, Travis Walton, claimed to have been captured and held for five days aboard a UFO. After he reappeared, he was given a lie-detector test, but failed it. The examiner concluded that Walton's story was false.

Unfortunately, this disappointing truth is that there are no authenticated reports of visits by alien spaceships. Whether or not there are any spacecraft traveling around the Galaxy at present, there will be one day. Those craft will be ours.

This strange object turned up on a photograph of a giraffe.

More than 90 percent of all UFO cases are solved. The main causes are misidentifications of bright stars and planets, aircraft, meteors (such as this daylight meteor streaking over Grand Teton, Wyoming) and satellites. A certain number are due to hallucinations and hoaxes. The information is not good enough to solve the remaining few percent of UFO cases. Not all crimes are solved, for the same reason.

FOR FURTHER READING

You will find the following books useful if you want to
learn more about any of the phenomena described on the previous pages.

ARDLEY, Neil *My Favourite Science Encyclopedia* Hamlyn, London 1984

ASIMOV, Isaac *Atoms* (How We Found Out About Series No. 6) Longman, Harlow 1982

ASIMOV, Isaac *Black Holes* (How We Found Out About Series No. 8) Longman, Harlow 1982

ASIMOV, Isaac *Comets* (How We Found Out About Series No. 15) Longman, Harlow 1983

ASIMOV, Isaac *Electricity* (How We Found Out About Series No. 13) Longman, Harlow 1983

ASIMOV, Isaac *Energy* (How We Found Out About Series No. 11) Longman, Harlow 1982

ASIMOV, Isaac *Outer Space* (How We Found Out About Series No. 1) Longman, Harlow 1982

BALFOUR, Michael *Stonehenge and Its Mysteries* (new edition) Hutchinson, London 1983

BLUNDELL, Nigel & BOAR, Roger *World's Greatest Unidentified Flying Objects Mysteries* Octopus Books, London 1984

COUPER, Heather & MURTAGH, Terence *Heavens Above!* Franklin Watts, London 1981

Hamlyn Junior Science Encyclopedia (2nd edition) Hamlyn, London 1985

DUNLOP, S. & WILSON, F. *The Country Life Guide to Weather Forecasting* Country Life Books, London 1982

HARDY, David *Air and Weather* (Advance of Science Series) World's Work, London 1977

HOLFORD, Ingrid (Editor) *Guinness Book of Weather Facts and Feats* (2nd edition) Guinness, London 1982

MOORE, Patrick *Guide to Comets* Lutterworth, Cambridge 1977

MOORE, Patrick (Editor) *The Guinness Book of Astronomy Facts and Feats* (2nd edition) Guinness, London 1983

MOORE, Patrick *Pocket Guide to the Stars and Planets* (2nd edition) Mitchell Beazley, London 1982

MOORE, Patrick *Unfolding Universe* Michael Joseph, London 1982

RIDPATH, Ian *Hamlyn Encyclopedia of Space* (2nd edition) Hamlyn, London 1985

RIDPATH, Ian *Life Off Earth* Granada, London 1983

RIDPATH, Ian *The Young Astronomer* Hamlyn, London 1985

RONAN, Colin *Amateur Astronomy* Newnes, London 1984

SNOWDEN, Sheila *The Young Astronomer* Usborne, London 1983

WHITE, T.M. WILDING- *U.F.O.s* (The World of the Unknown Series) Usborne, London 1977

WRIGHT, Peter (Editor) *The Weather Book* Michael Joseph, London 1982

Picture Acknowledgements

Anglo-Australian Observatory 46B, 54B; *Ann Ronan Picture Library* 35B, 40C; *Arecibo Observatory N.A.I.C. Cornell University* 60, 60T; *Courtesy of AT & T Bell Laboratories* 59B; *Janet & Colin Bord/*Fortean Picture Library 62BR, G. Ponting 15B; *Courtesy of British Aerospace/Dynamics Group, Bristol Division* 22B; *Canadian Forces Photo* 25BL, 25BR; *California Institute of Technology and Carnegie Institution of Washington* 34, 47B; *California Institute of Technology/Hale Observatory* 20B, 56B, 57BL/*Jet Propulsion Laboratory* 44B/*Palomar Observatory* 57BR; *A.P. Dowdell* 31; *Frank Lane Picture Library/*H. Binz 9B, J.D. Fernie 17C, 13B, C.D.R. Hill 12B, R. Maranges 13B, Naval Photo Centre 12B, Mrs. Otto 13T, A.A. Riley 10B, *Hamlyn Group Picture Library* 30, 46B; *M. Holford* 23T; *Huntington Library & Art Gallery* 59T; *Kitt Peak National Observatory* 51B, 56T; *Lick Observatory University of California, Santa Cruz* 21T, 48B, 53B; *Patrick Moore* 41B; *N.A.S.A.* 18C, 24B, 28, 29B, 32C, 35T, 37, 39, 40B, 41T, & C, 43C, 61T, 61B; *The National Gallery, London* 55T; *N.H.P.A./A.N.T./G.* McInnes 11T, 18B; *The National Portrait Gallery, London* 23B; *Photosources/ C.M. Dixon* 27T; *Courtesy of Province of Nova Scotia Information Office, London* 25BR, 26BL; *I. Ridpath* 17T, 35T, 43TL, California Institute of Technology 33, D. McLean 16, New Mexico State University Observatory 21C; *Royal Ob-servatory, Edinburgh* 47T, Anglo-Australian Observatory– D. Malin 51T; *Courtesy of Rutherford Appleton Laboratory* 44B; *Science Photo Library/*D. Allan 7T, J. Baker—D. Milan 62B; *Spacecharts/Robin Kerrod* 48B; *University of Hawaii at Manoa, Institute for Astronomy* 50B; *U.S. Naval Observatory Photograph* 55T; *Western Australian Newspapers* 24T, 24C; *Yerkes Observatory* 35B; *ZEFA Picture Library* 14B; J. Bitsch 11B, S. Warner 7B. With thanks to the Royal Astronomical Society, London.

Front cover

Science Photo Library (Lightning over Tucson, Arizona, USA): Inset top: A.F. Dowdell (Solar Eclipse); Inset Bottom: M. Holford (Detail from Bayeux Tapestry. Harold is told of the Comet.)

Back cover

Science Photo Library/Jack Finch (Auroral Arc, Fairbanks Alaska); Inset: Spectrum Colour Library (Stonehenge at Sunset).

Title page

Science Photo Library/Doug Johnson (Double rainbow).

Half-title page

Camerapix Hutchinson Library (Eclipse in Kenya (from color)).

INDEX

Page numbers referring to illustrations appear in *italics*